LITERACY PROJECTS
for
STUDENT-CENTERED CLASSROOMS

To my parents,
and to John and Henry Greene

LITERACY PROJECTS
for
STUDENT-CENTERED CLASSROOMS

TIPS AND LESSONS TO ENGAGE STUDENTS

KARRELL HICKMAN

CORWIN PRESS
A SAGE Publications Company
Thousand Oaks, CA 91320

For information:

Corwin Press
A Sage Publications Company
2455 Teller Road
Thousand Oaks, California 91320
www.corwinpress.com

Sage Publications Ltd.
1 Oliver's Yard
55 City Road
London EC1Y 1SP
United Kingdom

Sage Publications India Pvt. Ltd.
B 1/I 1 Mohan Cooperative
   Industrial Area
Mathura Road, New Delhi 110 044
India

Sage Publications Asia-Pacific Pte. Ltd.
33 Pekin Street #02-01
Far East Square
Singapore 048763

Printed in the United States of America

Library of Congress Cataloging-in-Publication Data

Hickman, Karrell.
Literacy projects for student-centered classrooms : tips and lessons to engage students / Karrell Hickman.
     p. cm.
Includes bibliographical references and index.
ISBN 978-1-4129-2450-4 (cloth)
ISBN 978-1-4129-2451-1 (pbk.)
   1. Language arts (Secondary) 2. Student-centered learning. I. Title.
LB1631.H49 2007

                              2006101265

This book is printed on acid-free paper.

07 08 09 10 11 10 9 8 7 6 5 4 3 2 1

Acquisitions Editor:	Allyson P. Sharp
Editorial Assistant:	Nadia Kashper
Production Editor:	Libby Larson
Copy Editor:	Teresa Herlinger
Typesetter:	C&M Digitals (P) Ltd.
Proofreader:	Theresa Kay
Indexer:	Pamela Onorato
Cover Designer:	Rose Storey
Graphic Designer:	Karine Hovsepian

Contents

Acknowledgments

I would like to thank Marlyn Pino-Jones and Jim Reidt for their dedication to education and the generous support they gave me when I taught at Bella Vista High. Many thanks also to Terry Healy for using my projects in her classroom and for her insights into a student-centered classroom. Thanks to John Elliott for reading and rereading my manuscript and for his copious list making; Kristin Gerry for her wonderful comments when reading my manuscript; Sally West for formatting my manuscript and supporting me through the publishing process from proposal to book; and last but not least, the many students who shared their ideas and creative energy with me.

Corwin Press would like to thank the following reviewers:

Jamie Jahnig, English Teacher
Cheyenne Central High School, Cheyenne, WY

Sonia T. Kelly, Director and Early Childhood Educator
Blue River Montessori School, Duxbury, MA

Joseph Meersman, Career and Technical Education Instructor
Toppenish High School, Toppenish, WA

Jonathan Plucker, Professor of Educational Psychology and
   Cognitive Science
Indiana University, Bloomington, IN

Jon Potter, Teacher of English and Drama
Camden Hills Regional High School, Rockport, ME

Kim C. Romero, National Board Certified English Teacher
Cumberland County Schools, Fayetteville, NC

Connie M. Stone, Education Specialist, NBPTS
Gadsden City High School, Gadsden, AL

Cathern Wildey, Literacy Specialist
Gulf High School, New Port Richey, FL

About the Author

 **Karrell Hickman** is a high school English teacher and is currently teaching at Feather River Academy in Yuba City, California. She has an MA in English and has been National Board Certified since 1995.

Introduction

At Open House this year, a mother suggested to me that my standards in English were too high and that I was "stressing" her daughter. She went on to say that she did not care if her daughter received a "B" in English, but in the next breath conceded that her daughter wanted an "A." I smiled, thinking to myself that the woman typified the confusing expectations our culture seems to have of public education.

Teachers are at the center of this fractured conversation. If you are a veteran, it is likely that you have experienced the cyclical nature of curricular reform (the same ideas pop up repackaged) and have weathered systemic change that, on balance, appears to only strengthen the traditional model of public education. We teachers are expected to perform miracles equaled only by the standardized test scores students are asked to achieve.

Nevertheless, the reality of the classroom is complex, carrying the subtle and persistent weight of the national dialogue while attempting to address the individual needs of its students. Tradition is an unspoken rule of thumb that both students and teachers understand only too well, and an attempt to change behavior often fails because, as students will tell you, "That is not how it is done." The irony, of course, is that students are begging for a different learning experience, although they have as much difficulty envisioning this change as the rest of us.

Add to that the complexity that high school teachers are typically responsible for five classes of students who run the gamut from reluctant learners to high achievers, some with special needs and others with limited English proficiency—the majority of whom are plugged into iPods or cell phones. In response to our students, we use our talents, life experience, and especially our preferences for our own teachers and learning environments to shape our instructional strategies.

My ideas for a student-centered classroom are loosely modeled after my experience in graduate school and nurtured by an ongoing dialogue with my students about boredom—which is the perennial catch word for a "state of being" when sitting, slouching, or sleeping in their seats. Student-centered behaviors are meant to be an antidote to this physical and psychological daze by expecting students to take responsibility for the learning environment so that it buzzes with activity.

My hope is to share ideas about student-centered behaviors and projects as a collaborative effort to create many high-interest projects and to expand and refine our expectations of students so that school moves them to learn. Chapter 1 provides teachers with some starter questions to reflect on their own instructional practices, and then explores student-centered behaviors that can be used within the context of individual activities or within the framework of a long-term project. Guidelines are provided for the design of student-led discussions, criteria, rubrics, and letters of evaluation for student self-assessment, and strategies are addressed that will encourage students to feel a sense of responsibility for their classmates through peer tutoring and group work.

Chapter 2 discusses how to map out a project that begins with one seminal idea and broadens to meet the needs of students with a variety of interests and learning styles. Suggested project topics are meant to inspire new teacher-generated projects and to have fun generating a list of topic ideas with colleagues.

Chapter 3 addresses project alignment with standards and the SCANS (Secretary's Commission on Achieving Necessary Skills) Report as a rationale for student-centered behaviors and the reality of high-stakes testing.

Chapters 4–7 are sample projects that I use in my classroom. I have provided teacher and student instructions with them in hopes that teachers can implement these projects or use them as templates for their own. I refer to the National Council of Teachers of English standards to support the projects, although the projects address standards in other subject areas as well.

In Chapter 8, there is a sampling of abbreviated case studies that will hopefully offer a sense of the quality and character of some aspects of student-centered behaviors and activities. The Resources section (Appendices A–E) contains sample worksheets to use or modify to fit your own project needs.

1

Working Toward a Student-Centered Classroom

There are enough students who feel little, if any, sense of "buy in" to the classroom learning experience that educators should have concerns. Unfortunately, what students feel is often overridden by what the general public and educators, in particular, specify as important. And yet, student compliance and real learning can be two distinct behaviors that seemingly overlap when students feel compelled to please parents and teachers. The most accomplished students will admit to boredom, although they usually push through it with great success and move on to other, more fulfilling experiences after high school. The fact that the federal government has to enumerate essential work-related skills that high school students need to know before entering the world of work (Secretary's Commission on Achieving Necessary Skills [SCANS], see Chapter 3 of this volume) confirms that we are ignoring a fundamental component of our students' education. The student-centered behaviors spelled out in this chapter are far from complete, but the bottom line is that students must experience the sense of responsibility that will be theirs after high school.

In elementary school, children take turns with tasks that actually mean something to classroom organization. For example, young students may change the date and time each day and present this to the class. Older students are often excluded from learning by doing. As students get older the focus is on book work within the academic classroom (plays, sports, clubs are acceptable ways for older students to be active). Middle and high school students work as teacher's aides, run errands, or help in the office under the watchful eye of adults but are not given any responsibility for what goes on in the classroom. The imbalance is best illustrated by the high school student who sleeps through the school day and then gets behind the wheel of a car and goes off to a job where he is expected to perform responsibly.

The first step in moving students toward responsibility for learning is to ask volunteers to lead classroom literature discussions. After much practice, these student-led discussions become standard classroom practice. When students lead them, they are energized, and the role reversal of student and teacher returns a spirited energy to the classroom where students show their academic knowledge, their ability to utilize social skills, and their sense of humor. It also creates a bond between student and teacher. And, despite careful planning on the part of the teacher, when students take center stage, there are bound to be surprises. These surprises are not about who misbehaves, but about a spontaneous moment when students really dig down to make meaning out of text or demonstrate their support for a classmate's idea.

In a year's time, these students are capable of making real strides in genuine classroom participation. From student-led discussions, students move to peer tutoring, developing criteria to evaluate assignments, and discussing how they will organize their time. With a lot of good-natured ribbing that only students can use with one another, the class begins to identify students who have trouble getting started on an assignment or sustaining it (time management issues that often cause students to give up), and they understand the need for peer tutors. Good peer tutors work carefully with their charges; it is a delicate relationship, and when it works, it is very powerful because it often helps to include students who feel marginalized.

While student-centered practices sound flawless, they are simply learning experiences and students, as well as the teacher, will have difficulty breaking old habits. At times, students will perceive their newfound freedom as a sign that their teacher is unable to control them and they may test the student-centered process to find boundaries. These are particularly good learning experiences for everyone, despite the fact that they can be tiring. Students resist classroom rules because they have very little stake in developing them. They can recite the rules, which are often too numerous, but would just as soon push at them than obey them. Over time, it will become clear even to students that their self-directed behavior is the foundation of a productive learning environment and that they need to practice these new behaviors and implement them with awareness.

Considering Your Instructional Practices

When thinking about what it means to change our instructional strategies and our attitudes toward our students, it is important not to misconstrue our role. At times, we will "stand and deliver" and we will discipline; but we will also actively cultivate a learning environment that moves students and ourselves beyond the prescriptive roles typical of the classroom.

A student-centered classroom is based on organized expectations orchestrated by the teacher and put into practice by students. Teachers are apt to learn as much as students throughout the process. It helps to understand our tolerance for multiple classroom activities, noise, and collaboration and to clarify our ideas about instructional strategies—which are often passionate.

Quick Tips for Considering Your Instructional Practices

- Take an honest look at your own "hot button" issues about teaching.
- In your view, is there only one correct way to teach?
- Do you feel in control of the classroom when you deliver the material?
- Do you consider yourself a flexible teacher?
- Do you accept suggestions from your students?
- Would you be willing to share some of the responsibility for instruction and assessment with your students?
- Do you develop the classroom rules and present them to your students, or do you work with your students to develop the classroom rules?
- Are you driven by content standards to cover a broad spectrum of subject material within the school year?
- If students study in depth by completing a project, do you believe the skills they learn are transferable?
- How do you assess whether your students understand concepts and are able to apply the skills they learn in your class to other activities?
- Do you find a new context to reteach students a concept or skill if your students are having difficulty?
- Would you be willing to team with your students to share responsibility for instruction, assessment, and behavior issues?
- In your view, what is the "perfect" student learning environment?
- What is the "perfect" instructional environment for teachers?
- What is your tolerance for noise and activity in the classroom?
- Are you comfortable juggling more than one activity in the classroom?
- What strategies do you use to sustain your interest in teaching?
- Would these strategies work to keep your students interested?
- Do you explore ideas about subject matter and instructional strategies with other educators?

Developing Student-Led
Class Discussions

Classroom discussions are familiar to students and are a good starting place to get them involved in assuming a leadership role in the classroom. One approach is to use question levels as the foundation of a discussion. To simplify the process, students use knowledge (recall), comprehension (understanding), and application (problem solving) questions and write their questions on different colored Post-its, which they stick to the board.

To understand question levels, the class reads a literature selection and develops a series of questions, which you can use as you teach. Students should focus on your teaching strategies—wait time, restating questions, and choosing a variety of students to answer them. When the class is comfortable, ask a student volunteer to lead the next discussion. The student leader very deliberately uses the student-generated question levels, and the class, in response, answers the questions and consciously supports the student discussion leader. Students must support their opinions with direct quotes from the text; they must prepare by noting page numbers so they can direct the class quickly to the correct page.

An alternative discussion strategy uses a reading or dialectical journal as the basis of a discussion. Reading journals allow students to express their likes and dislikes about what they are reading, make connections between a literature selection and popular culture, note interesting quotes, and isolate difficult vocabulary. In a dialectical journal, students identify challenging quotes to explicate. Both types of journals slow down the reading pace as students interact with the text.

Students should think of these carefully orchestrated discussions as assignments. Everyone is required to participate and actively listen. It is common to assume that students understand what it means to listen, but in actuality, they are often after our approval and are focused on being the first student to be called upon to answer a question. Because of this habit, make "listening" the focus of a number of discussions. This means that students are required to acknowledge a classmate's idea before presenting their own. If they have difficulty understanding what the discussion leader or a classmate is saying, they must ask for clarification. Listening intently typically slows the discussion down (as does finding quotes from the text) and sometimes it even stops it, but ultimately students will be able to build on each other's ideas.

Quick Tips for a Student-Led Class Discussion

- Develop a thematic unit of essays, short stories, and poems for your class to explore, using student-led discussions.
- Introduce and practice "questioning" strategies.
- Model how to lead a discussion using questions generated by students.
- Use a student volunteer to lead a discussion, using question levels.
- Ask students to prepare for a student-led discussion using a reading or dialectical journal.
- Underscore the importance of listening strategies and class support for the student-discussion leader.
- Practice listening strategies until students are able to build on each other's ideas.

The Logistics of Whole-Class, Student-Led Discussions

Student-led discussions should occupy the class hour. The first 5 minutes of class are used for preparation. Ten minutes are reserved for evaluation (reserve another 5 minutes for your feedback if it is needed), and another 5 minutes are set aside to assign roles for the following day's discussion. The timekeeper in this instance has an important role, although he or she may still participate in the discussion. Once the roles of leader, evaluator, and timekeeper have been established, the class prepares for the discussion. The leader will feel much the way we do as teachers when preparing a lesson, and students who rarely do homework will prepare because they are responsible for making the discussion work. The class understands that the success of the discussion relies on a careful reading of the literature and the use of specific strategies for explication (questions, journals, quotes from the text). They also understand that their participation supports the student leader, and their sensitivity to other students' ideas helps build a safe environment.

The evaluator remains outside the discussion and takes notes. When the discussion is over, the evaluator stands in front of the class and, using student-generated discussion criteria (see the Building Criteria section below), focuses on the discussion process. Students may question or respond to the evaluator's comments, and often the dialogue between the evaluator and the class becomes a valuable learning tool.

During the discussion, don't let the class or the discussion leader make eye contact with you. They are in the habit of looking to the teacher for answers and will fall back into this pattern even if they are determined to avoid your input. Take notes so that you can provide feedback after the evaluator has finished commenting on the discussion.

It is not difficult to identify moments when students appear to need help during a discussion. Sometimes the leader has difficulty moving the discussion on to a new topic. If the student leader does not repeat ideas so that the students can hear, the discussion will stop, and if the class genuinely cannot make sense of a literature passage, then you will need to step in. It is important not to do this too quickly, however. Students need time to wrestle with concepts to make sense of them.

An alternative approach to a single student discussion leader is to use a pair of students. This works well in a whole-class discussion because while one student teaches, the other repeats questions and student answers and generally makes sure everyone can hear. Halfway through the discussion, students exchange roles. This strategy also works for shy students who are uncomfortable standing in front of the class by themselves.

Quick Tips for Whole-Class, Student-Led Discussions

- Develop discussion criteria with the class and display them on the classroom wall.
- Use volunteers for the initial discussions; agree upon the literature selection.
- Assign student roles: discussion leader, timekeeper, and evaluator.
- Review time requirements for the discussion hour.
- Allow students to be independent of your participation and feedback as long as they can handle the responsibility.
- Let the evaluator provide discussion feedback before you give yours.
- Break the class hour into segments and write them on the board to help the class and especially the timekeeper.

Small-Group, Student-Led Discussions

Small-group, student-led discussions are more personal than class discussions. Students feel a sense of pride when they are able to discuss without teacher interference, and it is clearer to them how to assist their classmates. The spirit of these discussions is to make sure that everyone in the group understands the literature, and each group member can pitch in to make this happen. Student groups prepare for a discussion by reading a literature selection the night before, noting important ideas and page numbers. Short poems work well for first discussions and fit nicely into 15-minute segments.

Designate a discussion table in your room and divide students into groups of 5 to 8 students. Each group takes a turn at the table, and the remainder of the class either listens to the discussion or completes an alternative assignment while waiting for their turn.

The day before discussions begin, group members identify a leader, timekeeper, and an evaluator. The leader is responsible for posing the initial question about the literature selection, eliciting responses from group members, and checking for understanding. If the group is stuck, the leader moves them on to another idea. Each group member is required to participate and encouraged to ask questions if he or she does not understand.

The timekeeper is a member of the discussion group but has the added responsibility of warning the group when it is 5 minutes before the end of the discussion. The evaluator, on the other hand, is not a group member and sits outside the discussion taking notes and observing. After the discussion is over, the evaluator has 5 minutes to provide feedback about the discussion using the criteria the class has developed for small-group discussions.

Your role is to observe from a distance and listen for ideas about the literature you feel need correcting or expanding. Try not to nod your head or make eye contact with students as they discuss. They are in the habit of looking to you for answers rather than struggling to make meaning on their own. Intervene in a discussion only if students sincerely need your help or ask for it. If you are asked to sit in on a discussion, remember that the student leader is still responsible for the discussion.

It is natural to fear that students will miss important points when the discussions are turned over to them. But for the most part, students seem to unravel issues at their own pace and in their own words. Discussions are congruent with student experience, but they are also sprinkled with the technical terms we have taught them to use when discussing writing and literature. There is a surprising sense of discovery during the best student discussions, and students often generate and answer their own questions.

If there is time, videotape the discussions. Students may feel some initial embarrassment with the camera focused on them, but it won't take long before they are coming in at lunch to view their discussion.

Quick Tips for Small-Group, Student-Led Discussions

- The day before a discussion, pick a literature selection.
- Divide the class into groups of 5–8 students.
- Ask each group to choose a leader, timekeeper, and evaluator.
- Clarify roles and responsibilities.
- Encourage students to focus on a specific behavior or academic idea during the discussion.

(Continued)

Quick Tips (Continued)

- Work with your class to develop the criteria for small-group discussions and display them in the classroom where they can be seen.
- Arrange discussion group order.
- Write appropriate time limits on the board.

On the day of the discussion, do the following:

- Set up a discussion table.
- Provide the class with an alternate assignment to complete while discussions are in progress.
- Limit discussions to 15 minutes, with an additional 5 minutes for the evaluator's feedback.
- Observe discussions, but do not interfere unless students ask for your help.
- Listen to the evaluator's assessment of the discussion before providing your feedback.
- Videotape discussions.

Building Criteria

Building criteria for a student-led discussion (as well as other assignments) helps students internalize what is expected of them. Criteria for a student-led discussion should consider the effectiveness of the leader and the level of participation by group members. The whole class contributes to the development of discussion criteria, and a student writes these ideas on the board or on a piece of butcher paper. Once the class has developed a list of criteria, let the list alone for a day, and then ask your class to review and refine it. As students become proficient at student-led discussions, they will continue to improve the criteria.

Students can also focus on one goal during a discussion. When my students were practicing their first small-group discussions, they were determined to conduct them without my intervention. Students actively pursued this goal, playing it like a game, and I did not discourage them. Here is how they wrote the criteria:

Students

- Rely heavily on the teacher to generate the discussion,
- Combine efforts with the teacher to generate the discussion,
- Carry the discussion with little or no help from the teacher.

Later, students broadened the discussion criteria:

- The leader gives each student an opportunity to speak.
- The leader clarifies ideas and keeps the discussion moving.
- Group members listen and acknowledge individual student ideas.
- Students ask questions of each other and listen carefully before responding.
- Students support their ideas with specific passages from the literature.

Note: The criteria from class to class may be similar, but each class needs to develop their own set of criteria to own them.

A more sophisticated version of a small-group, student-led discussion is to ask students to focus on a theme in a novel. My seniors broke into groups of 6 to 8 students and picked a theme from *Cry, the Beloved Country* as their focus. They spent several class periods researching the historical background of South Africa, keeping a reading journal, and meticulously noting page numbers of ideas relating to their theme.

Each group chose a leader, evaluator, researcher, and timekeeper. The researcher had the job of beginning the discussion by providing background information on the history of South Africa as it related to the novel. Discussions and the evaluator's comments were video-taped in the television studio at our high school. Students developed the following criteria for the discussion.

Small-Group Discussion Criteria for a Novel

Discussion Process:

- There is evidence of a team effort.
- The conversation is genuine and spontaneous.
- The facilitator moves the discussion along.
- The timekeeper keeps the group on schedule.
- Team members have many opportunities to speak.

Academic Content:

- There is evidence that group members read the novel and kept a reading journal.
- Members of the group prepared thoughtful questions and insights based on the group's chosen theme.
- Ideas are supported by quotes and examples from the text.
- Factual data are clearly represented (i.e., character and geographical names are correctly identified).

- Group members acknowledge differing points of view by listening and clarifying.

This discussion worked well because these students had the maturity to prepare for the discussion independently of the teacher for the most part. They were sensitive to individual group members and were able to highlight the subtleties of the literature.

Quick Tips for Developing Discussion Criteria

- Use the overhead to review with students the expectations for the assignment.
- Use the students' general knowledge about writing, speaking, and so forth, to develop a list of criteria that can be refined later.
- Use what students have specifically learned from studying a topic and develop a list of criteria that can be refined later.
- Pass out a student model of criteria on a topic so that they can learn to use the appropriate language when developing their criteria.
- Develop the criteria as a class using the overhead or a student recorder, or break the class into groups to work on criteria that later can be combined.
- Develop criteria for both student behavior and academic content.
- Make the final list of criteria short and to the point.

From Criteria to Rubrics: Student-Led Assessment Tool

Student-generated rubrics are meant to be a part of the learning process, and with the help of them, the requirements for any assignments become clear. Over the years, my classes have developed rubrics for essays, presentations, speeches, and literature packets (portfolios). I do not try to refine them after students feel they are complete unless there is a glaring omission. The process is lengthy and requires an eye for detail, and I don't want to discourage them.

A rubric is a roadmap, and if students create it, they cannot help but understand what is expected of them. Rubrics emphasize skill mastery rather than grades, which is a relief to everyone. Typically, students have a sense of how well they performed on an assignment, although they may not be able to identify why. Rubrics provide this information for them—and it is difficult to argue with a rubric students themselves created.

Sample Criteria for a Reflective Essay

The following criteria were built by a class of seniors working on writing a reflective essay. They analyzed the essays of both student and professional writers, and through student-taught mini lessons, identified the essay's component parts. Using the appropriate terms to discuss these essays (an anecdotal introduction, personal and universal reflection, and new awareness) was a powerful tool in the development of their own essays.

- Use of narrative (too much, too little)
- Varied sentence structure and vocabulary
- Grammatical errors and structural problems
- Punctuation and mechanics
- Organization and flow of essay
- Clarity of ideas and supportive details
- Presence of writer's voice
- Use of clichés
- Explanation of ideas
- Insufficient reflection
- The writer's movement from personal to universal reflection
- Evidence of a new awareness

The criteria were then developed into a rubric, which went through several brainstorming sessions in class and three major rewrites.

Student-Generated Reflective Essay Rubric

Mastery

Clear and concise presentation (clarity)

Strong writer's voice and style

Writer keeps audience in mind

Writer-developed reflection with a personal and universal connection

Varied sentence structure and vocabulary

Good mechanics and grammar

Effective conclusion

Strong new awareness by end of essay

Proficiency

Lacks complete clarity but is easy to read

Writer's voice somewhat present, but not necessarily strong

Needs more explanation of ideas

Has personal reflection but doesn't necessarily relate it to the universal

Narrative is strong but could be shortened

Few grammatical errors and structural problems

Conclusion has new awareness, but it could be clarified

Basic Skills

Little clarity; leaves reader confused

Weak writer's voice

Ideas are not fully developed; lacks sufficient personal insight

Has insufficient reflection, too much narrative, and little detail or support

Many grammatical errors and inconsistent structure

Unvaried vocabulary and too many clichés

Unclear conclusion; leaves loose ends

Flaws in organization; circular flow in narrative and reflection

No new awareness

Other Sample Student-Generated Rubrics

After participating in several student-led discussions, the class experimented with practicing "listening" as a skill. This exercise helped students slow down and acknowledge each other during discussions and eventually led to a "listening" rubric. This rubric made a dramatic difference in the pacing of these discussions.

Student-Led Class Discussion Rubric (Listening)

Mastery:

Students

Acknowledge the ideas of a classmate before speaking,

Pay attention to discussion details and take notes,

Are courteous and respectful during a discussion,

Ask questions to clarify an idea.

Students and discussion leader

Demonstrate a progressively clearer understanding of the material.

Discussion leader

Restates the idea being discussed.

Proficiency:

Students

Listen most of the time,

Occasionally interrupt a speaker,

Take notes so they will not forget a discussion idea.

Students and discussion leader

Are courteous most of the time,

Often use specific listening strategies.

Discussion leader

Occasionally moves the discussion too quickly,

At times forgets to repeat ideas so the class can hear.

Basic skills:

Students

Pay attention only when they are asked to respond,

Do not take notes to catch the details of discussion,

Do not acknowledge a classmate's idea before speaking,

Sleep or appear bored during the discussion.

Students and discussion leader

Are unable to listen without interrupting.

Discussion leader

Is nervous and unprepared to guide the discussion.

Quality: Using Members of the School Community

If students develop a rubric that moves from basic skills to mastery, then there will be students who will work to master the material. This is especially true of students who are giving presentations and speeches. If they are determined to reach mastery, they will find audiences of counselors, administrators, and other classes are all fair game. The student provides the audience with a rubric and is evaluated, sometimes three or four times, by different classes and individuals on campus. After presenting to their class, students may arrange to present in other teachers' classrooms or for a counselor or administrator. The number of presentations a student gives depends upon his or her determination to master the presentation. An administrator who has the time to hear even one student's speech makes a big impression.

Quick Tips for Creating Rubrics

- Allow plenty of time for your class to create a rubric.
- Help your class understand that a rubric is a detailed road map of an assignment.
- Pass out sample rubrics to the class.
- Encourage class to use the language in the sample rubrics to develop their own.
- Break class into groups to work on a rubric.
- Combine group rubrics into a class rubric by using the overhead and a student scribe.
- Listen to students as they discuss, and coach them by asking questions to improve the clarity of the final rubric.
- Don't expect a student rubric to be as refined as one created by teachers.
- Ask for volunteers to refine the final class rubric and present it to the class for suggestions.
- Allow students to refine the rubric when they begin to use it as an assessment tool.

Other Assessment Tools

Letter of Evaluation

The letter of evaluation is a good method of bringing a semester or a project to a close. Students write a formal letter addressed to you, reviewing their academic performance as well as their participation in student-centered activities. To support their assessment of their performance, they must quote from old assignments, address peer and teacher evaluations, and reflect on skills they are proud of and areas that need improving. This is an instance where students often do not know what they know until they write it. You will enjoy reading these letters, and they will anticipate your comments (see outline of letter of evaluation in Appendix A).

Quick Tips for Writing Letters of Evaluation

- Work with your students to develop a list of assignments they completed during a semester or project.
- List titles of novels, essays, short stories, and poems the class studied.
- List specific skills that were reviewed or introduced (e.g., punctuation, documentation).
- List student-centered behaviors the class practiced.
- Provide students with a formal letter format.
- Decide whether the letter will be written in class or at home.
- Ask students to evaluate a project or specific assignment if you want the feedback.
- Remind students to save their class work so they can use it when writing their letter.

Other Informal Evaluations

Maintaining the quality of student work is directly related to how well students understand what is expected of them. Discussing what it means to produce "quality" is an essential part of the process of prethinking the criteria for an assignment. Students can and should evaluate drafts of essays, graphics, and presentations. They should evaluate other classroom and group behaviors beyond student-led discussions. Help students to be aware of their habits when visiting the library, setting up for group work, or visiting the campus television studio. When preparing for a presentation in the theater or choir room, ask them to consider the issue of "trust" and what it means to meet their commitments. Tie these discussions to prior experiences when they were responsible for a task either at school or for an organization in the community.

Tutors, Teachers, and Collaborators

Peer Tutoring

Ask for volunteer peer tutors in your classes at the beginning of the year and meet with them to discuss strategies that they can use to help their classmates. It is a good idea to ask them to commit to working with a student over a specific period of time. Of course, if the responsibility proves too much, then they should stop. Most often it helps both students focus and encourages friendships that might not otherwise occur.

Peer tutors can help struggling students just by having a daily conversation with them. My tutors typically do not let their charges get away with anything. They insist that the student open the textbook and that he or she is prepared with pencil and paper at the beginning of each class period. Both students write out the assignment, but they may work together to complete it.

Recognize peer tutors with extra credit, calls home to parents, letters of recommendation, or acknowledgment during a school program.

Peer Teaching (Mini Lessons)

Peer teaching is not meant to be complex or responsibility laden. It is simply another tool for encouraging student participation and has the added bonus of encouraging students to learn from each other. It also provides students with an opportunity to see subject matter from the perspective of a teacher, which means that the student is using critical thinking and organizational skills.

When a student prepares a lesson, the focus should be on teaching an isolated skill, such as use of semicolons, or demonstrating a process to master a difficult skill. For example, a student might demonstrate the process he or she followed to arrive at a solid thesis statement.

Provide the student with "teacher" material and encourage the use of the overhead. Instruction using transparencies is a systematic approach that shapes the lesson and ensures that the class will have a visual example. Review the peer teacher's lesson and suggest ways he or she might encourage class participation during the lesson. Classes often respond eagerly to a peer teacher. It is an opportunity for them to explore what they know about a subject (often one they have learned and relearned over their years in English class) without being guided by an adult. Peer teaching, when it works, seems to wake up students to their potential as independent learners.

Peer teaching may sound time consuming, but in reality, students who volunteer to teach have usually led discussions and feel comfortable speaking in front of the class. It is not necessary to turn a peer teacher into a student teacher, but it is possible to make simple suggestions about instruction; for example, allowing for "wait time" and speaking to students on both sides of the classroom. When the class is involved in a project, these lessons, as well as your own, are embedded into the project.

A subtle form of peer teaching occurs when students direct their classmates to Web sites or reference material they have come across in the course of their research or share practical information such as library hours, professional contacts, and phone numbers. Designate a bulletin board for this purpose and ask a student volunteer to update it.

Giving Back to the School and Other Challenge Projects

There will be teachers who are willing to work with you to allow students to peer teach in their classrooms. Arrange opportunities for seniors to teach a short story or an essay to a freshman or sophomore class. Giving back to the school is rewarding, and seniors especially enjoy participating before they graduate.

Design other challenge assignments for students who complete their work at a faster pace or have a particular interest they wish to pursue in more depth. Students typically stumble on ideas for challenge assignments when they are immersed in research.

Quick Tips for Peer Teaching

- Peer teaching includes tutoring, teaching mini lessons, sharing research information, and teaching a literature selection to a class of younger students.
- Peer teachers should concentrate on teaching isolated skills: punctuation review, editing, revision, formatting or documentation, or sharing a personal process for mastering a skill.
- It is appropriate to follow up with a lesson to expand on the ideas that the peer teacher presented.
- Challenge seniors to give back to their school by teaching a lesson to a younger class of students.
- Ask colleagues to participate in the peer teaching process by allowing your students to share a lesson with their class.

Time Management

Managing time is a challenge for many students, and they will admit they have trouble using their time well. In the classroom, it can be very frustrating for a teacher to find a powerful enough rationale to motivate students to get their work done. Many students feel little intrinsic need to comply with the expectations of teachers. They lack the motivation to learn what is presented to them, not because it is necessarily "boring," but because they are passive participants in the learning process. There is a daily tug-of-war that students and teachers act out in the classroom. Teachers ask students to utilize their time efficiently, and students rebel, sometimes overtly, although often, the behavior is routine—students forget to bring the proper learning tools, such as paper, pencil, and book.

Empowerment for students comes with having a stake in the learning process, and this is an essential ingredient to making a long-term project a success. In the beginning stages of a project, time management manifests itself through a variety of learning styles. A handful of students will have so many ideas that they cannot settle on one; other students will put off the research necessary to arrive at a suitable topic; and others will systematically knock off each assignment until they have accomplished them all.

It is important to put a time management strategy in place that gives students an opportunity to plan how they will use each week during a long-term project. This process found its natural place in my classroom, when on Mondays we decided what work was necessary to complete over the course of the week. On Fridays, we reevaluated and decided what could be accomplished over the weekend. Weekend work was not my idea. It was inspired by students who saw opportunities on weekends to use their time in a college library or to interview someone. This is the sense of empowerment you want your students to experience.

Students also should have input in making decisions about due dates. We are used to students trying to persuade us to move back a due date, but that is because they see us as having the power to make these decisions. Involve them in the process and they will arrive at a very reasonable consensus—and this is what will save your sanity as a teacher. The handful of students who will express an outrageous due date will be overridden by the majority. In fact, students are often harder on themselves than I would have been on them.

Calendars

During a project, supply students with a blank calendar to record what they accomplish daily (see "Blank Calendar" in Appendix A). When the class discusses what has been accomplished during the week or what project should be accomplished, a calendar is the map that helps them visualize their progress. Make a transparency of the calendar to show students on the overhead as you explain the project. Provide students with their own calendar to copy the general project timeline from your transparency. Use calendars for weekly review of important dates and changes made to the timeline throughout the project. Keep a stack of them on hand for student use. At the end of a project, students can review their accomplishments and use this information in their letter of evaluation.

Proposals

Proposals are an optional activity. They are a written plan that students produce to explain and explore a project idea. In their proposal, students provide an idea or thesis, identify problems they foresee, and explain how they propose to solve them. Proposals are especially helpful to students who have trouble committing to a project idea. They are also useful when students plan to use community resources.

Examples of proposals can be found in any technical writing textbook and can be adapted to suit your purpose.

Progress Memos

A progress memo is an excellent way for students to give you an update on their project progress. While they will do this verbally as well, there are times when you are too busy to consider individual needs. A memo is something you can read and consider later when you have time to really think about what the student is saying.

Progress memos are formatted like a business memo. Students briefly describe what they are working on, ask questions, or discuss a problem. Memos are short and easy to read. Use colored paper and copy four memos to a sheet, back and front. Students can continue to use them and keep them in their notebook (see sample "Progress Memo" in Appendix A).

Outside Reading

There will be days when you and your students will need a break from a project, and outside reading is a restful way to ease stress. Require students to carry an outside reading book in their backpacks. They may read fiction or nonfiction, and if they maintain a reading journal or dialectical journal (develop a reading journal with students and their task in mind), and finish reading their book, they receive credit (see "Dialectical Journal" in Appendix A).

For students who have completed a project assignment and arrive in class with nothing to do, outside reading is a good backup and will relieve you of the need to create busywork.

Pacing

Students are required to keep pace with the general expectations for a project during any given week, but within these perimeters, the pacing between students may differ. It is possible that some students will need more library time and others will need to type in the computer lab. Perhaps a student has set up an interview with a history teacher during the teacher's prep time. Students can accomplish these activities at lunch, or before or after school, but it is reasonable to allow them to take care of some of these tasks during class time.

Prepare the librarian, computer teacher, hall monitors, and any other adults who might encounter your students outside of your classroom. Work with students to develop the behaviors necessary to trust them to move around campus without supervision. This arrangement benefits everyone. It satisfies students who want to get things done and will give you time to work with students in the classroom who need extra help. Students who cannot handle this independence must remain in the classroom.

Course Correcting

Projects are refined each time you implement them. The first time through, the flaws in your thinking will become apparent. Modify assignments, listen to student feedback, and make practical decisions that will benefit everyone.

Quick Tips for Time Management

- Review the project with the class.
- Ask students to write a project proposal (optional).
- Pass out a blank calendar to each student.
- Discuss assignment expectations for the week on Mondays.
- Discuss weekend work every Friday.
- Check calendars periodically to make sure students are recording their progress and planning their time wisely.
- Set aside days for students to work or read quietly in the classroom.
- Prepare the librarian, computer teacher, and hall monitor to receive your students.
- Send students to the library or computer lab, and keep the remaining students in the classroom.
- Embed student-led discussions, class discussions, and mini lessons as the need arises.
- Make sure you and your students agree on due dates and then stick to them.
- Modify assignments, add ideas, and listen to students.

Considering Lessons and Lesson Planning

When students have become comfortable using student-centered behaviors during class lessons, it is time to transition to a research project. A good research project piques student interest, allows a student some leeway to make a topic choice within a broader context, and is driven by essential questions. For example, a class of seniors could be required, at the end of the year, to write and deliver a graduation speech to the class. Students will be interested in this topic because they are graduating, and it is an opportunity for them to reflect upon their high school experience and their future. This is the emotional hook that will get them interested. As a teacher, however, you will want them to discuss something of substance and avoid the traditional clichés associated with graduation. Give them the latitude to look backward and forward personally, but also require that they reflect upon a contemporary issue that affects their generation; for example, a war, civil rights, a Supreme Court decision, an election, or an environmental or technological issue. By insisting on a substantive issue, the graduation speech is significantly transformed and now becomes a research project.

The student-centered behaviors help students move through the research process, from the development of essential questions to the citing of sources, as well as the process of writing and revising the speech and practicing its delivery. Peer teaching and tutoring become a powerful tool for the mastery and application of skills; working in small groups provides peer support to sustain research and acknowledge and overcome any frustrating dead ends. Students are involved in the development of criteria or a rubric for evaluating the speeches and may choose to attain mastery by giving their speech to other classes or to a member of the administrative staff.

The teacher's job is to provide the project framework and clear expectations. Working to support students and receiving feedback from students offer opportunities to refine a project and to avoid some of the pitfalls the next time through. It is truly a rewarding team effort.

2

How to Create a Project

Creating a student-centered project will renew your interest in teaching and generate excitement in the classroom. It has the effect of releasing students and teachers from the traditional method of delivery and response. It is a team effort and everyone learns.

Where to Find Project Ideas

Use a variety of material—textbooks, newspapers, library books, and the Internet—to find suitable project topics.

Since textbooks are arranged thematically, each unit has the potential to become a project because the initial literature connections are made for you. Gauging student interest and talent (many students are musical or artistic) is another way to hit upon a good project topic. Allowing for diverse research paths helps students extend their understanding of subjects they have studied in other classes. Writers become human through biographical information and life stories that demonstrate the connections among history, science, and the arts and their influence on literature.

Project Ideas

View projects as a way for students to see literature from a creative perspective. Use maps, recipes, old news articles, music, dance, and fashion to tap the personal interests of students. Use a broad stroke when creating a project so that students who are strong in history, science, and even math can find a research path that interests them. For example, students may

- Ride a steamboat down the Mississippi with Mark Twain;
- Join Anne Moody at Woolworth's lunch counter to protest segregation;
- Develop a psychological profile of a soldier returning home from Vietnam;
- Sit with Thoreau at Walden Pond;
- Interview the characters of Garrison Keillor's *Lake Wobegon* to examine American attitudes about work, relationships, religion, and the delicacies of the tuna and noodle casserole;
- Examine the influence of women in a Faulkner novel;
- Walk the Muir trail using maps and the writings of John Muir to discover the High Sierras;
- Travel with the cowboys in a Larry McMurtry novel to discover the American West;
- Enter the mind of Ethan Frome as his psychiatrist;
- Explore the natural world as seen through the eyes of Annie Dillard in *Pilgrim at Tinker Creek* and connect it to an issue in science;
- Draw a map of the Southwest based on a Tony Hillerman mystery and research the traditions of the Navajo and other Native American cultures;
- Examine famous proclamations of love found in letters and poems in British literature;
- Develop a theatrical piece in which three authors discuss their most famous essays (e.g., Woolf, Orwell, Swift);
- Perform famous monologues from plays based on a theme.

A Sample Research Project to Fit an Occasion

It is also possible to focus a project on a specific occasion—employment, college applications, volunteer work, or graduation—to celebrate a meaningful event in students' lives.

Graduation Speech

All seniors should have the chance to give a graduation speech before leaving high school. This is a powerful way for a senior class to end the year. Individual students research a newsworthy topic that will affect their generation as they enter the adult world. Topics may include the environment, alternative fuel sources, technology, family, and war, among others. Students begin their speech with a personal anecdote about their school years and then focus on their research topic. The speech must be reflective and well crafted. Students are required to avoid clichés with a vengeance, and keep this thought in mind when they listen to the actual graduation speeches on the night of their graduation (see "Graduation Speech Worksheet" in Appendix A).

Lesson Versus Project

Some ideas are better left as lessons rather than projects. One day in class, students were presenting English and Spanish versions of an excerpt from the poem "I Am Joaquin" by Rodolfo Gonzales. The class enjoyed the sound of fluent Spanish and the Spanish speakers in the class were validated by the experience. I was inspired to turn this lesson into a bilingual project, but the limitation is obvious—not all students are bilingual and every student needs to have access to the project.

Incorporating Important Language Concepts

Here are some suggestions to help students understand the importance of technical language skills and provide them with an opportunity to practice and apply them:

- Embed the practice of reading, writing, speaking, and listening into the project.
- Think of punctuation and usage as a "need-to-know" activity to complete the project.
- Make writing and refining thesis statements a class activity.
- Require students to use technical terms when discussing literature and writing.
- Explore the influence of history, science, and the humanities on literature.

The Design

Project design needs to be broad enough to accommodate a variety of interests and kinds of learners. The musical *South Pacific*, for instance, has the potential to be a strong class project because of its social message about racial prejudice; the historical origins and audience response to a musical with a controversial message; the catchy lyrics; and, of course, the music, which is a big draw for adolescents. Although in another context, students might think watching the movie version of *South Pacific* to be a bore, as the foundation of a class project, it can be an effective "hook," despite the fact that it is not the racy, fast-paced visual experience they get on television or at the movies.

The basis for translating *South Pacific* into a research project is in the development of a worthy thesis—which, in high school, is a lengthy and challenging process that is crafted through much peer review and teacher feedback. The research itself takes students into the history and culture of the times, and the lyrics provide a motif that runs throughout the research. There is nothing as compelling or straightforward as "You've got to be taught/To hate and fear," and adolescents can easily relate to this message.

There is plenty of room for embedding skill-based lessons and integrating student-centered behaviors within the context of the project, and certainly in the culminating experience of presentations, speeches, monologues, skits, and so forth, required at the end of a project to demonstrate what students have learned and to share it with the class. Each sample project provides a list of ideas for possible culminating experiences. These generate a great deal of excitement because they provide students with a venue for their own talents as musicians, singers, actors, storytellers, and producers, and also give them an opportunity to share these talents with other students.

Considering the Parameters of Your Project

You might answer the following questions to determine if the parameters of the project are appropriate for your class:

- Is your project broad enough to allow for some independent student choice?
- Will it address the needs of students with remedial skills and those who need a challenge?
- Can you modify it for English language learners and younger students?
- Will your project interest teens and draw on talents they might not otherwise use in an English classroom?
- Does your project show a relationship to other subjects—art, music, history, science?
- Does your project allow for the practice and application of language arts skills described in the standards?
- Is it based on research and does it provide opportunities for students to explore ideas and develop critical thinking skills?
- Can you envision how students might use student-centered behaviors during a project to explore ideas and support one another?
- Can students share their projects with the class and other students on campus?

Reversing the Process: High Interest First

Sometimes the way to draw in high school students is to present something so interesting or so lacking in their lives that they forget their resistance to school work and become eager to go to work. At the end of the year, I asked my alternative school students to compile their best assignments in a portfolio. We discussed what it meant to do quality work while developing criteria and identified assignments that met a variety of standards. Students were reluctant to begin revising and assembling work for their portfolio, protesting that they didn't see the point in improving work that they had already completed.

The next day, I experimented with reversing the process and proposed to the class that they develop a cover for their portfolios first. I brought in sample work by former students—an illustration, a cover made of newspaper headlines, and a collage I'd made the night before from ribbons and wrapping paper. Along with these creative samples, I showed them formal cover pages typed by students who had completed research papers. We discussed the possibilities for covers, listened as a few resistors declared artwork stupid, and then the majority of students began to work.

The art supplies I provided were cheap, but varied. Students admired the stickers, colored paper, and so forth, and worked as if they were in elementary school. Over the week, many of them redid their covers. When I offered students notebooks to put their work in, a number of them rejected the offer because they were used. Around this time, it started to dawn on them that they needed to revise and rewrite their assignments so that their work would be equal to the quality of their covers.

When they completed their portfolios, they were eager to evaluate the quality of their work and even improve upon it. They had a context for understanding quality work, and the artwork was the "hook" that provided the internal motivation to complete the project.

Combining Academic and Technical Classes for a Hands-on Project

Given the cyclical nature of educational philosophy, ideas that once reached a segment of our student population are often replaced by another trend. Currently, technical programs and shop classes have been reduced or phased out and replaced by intensive "skill and drill" to ensure that students pass multiple standardized tests.

While not all students who enroll in shop classes have trouble seeing the relevance of academic classes, there are enough that do. They are typically "hands-on" learners who solve problems through experimentation, who apply their skills to rebuild a carburetor or cut someone's hair.

Combining a shop class with a core class such as English allows students to experience firsthand the connection between two seemingly very different activities. A student deeply involved in small engine repair who learns to read technical manuals and write reports has found a match between technical and academic skills. There is a solid rationale for providing students with this learning environment and the projects that can be developed are unlimited.

Scheduling is typically problematic when linking an academic and a shop class to develop projects, and sometimes it is easier to bring hands-on projects into the academic classroom. For example, essays and stories about "flight" are often included in textbooks. Using flight as a theme, students may write a proposal to build gliders in the English classroom and develop instruction manuals as they work.

Organizing

Projects that span six to eight weeks require an organizational system like the portfolio so that teachers can monitor student work and students can display their work. Organizing a project also allows the teacher to respond to assignments as they are completed (rather than waiting until the end). Giving immediate feedback to students helps them sustain the project and allows them to rework assignments.

Develop a template to use for writing out project assignments. Procedures should be clear, and students should have an opportunity to use checklists to complete their work (see sample "Project Format" in Appendix A). Block out a tentative project calendar to present to the class at the inception of the project and adjust it as you receive feedback from the students (see "Blank Calendar" in Appendix A).

Involve students in planning and the development of schedules for certain assignments. In Appendix A, there is a schedule (the "Sample Student Scheduling Graphic") developed by students for learning to edit videotape in the television studio. The schedule divides students into groups of teachers (those who know how to edit) and students (those who need to learn). Dates, times, and names of teachers and students are typed and copied onto an overhead so the class can easily refer to them.

Culminating Activities

Culminating activities provide students with an opportunity to share what they have learned and to utilize their talents. It is gratifying to find the musicians, actors, and artists among our students and include their gifts in a classroom activity. Make the culminating activity an event that students look forward to experiencing, and allow them to share this activity with other classes on campus.

Worksheets

Use worksheets to reinforce skills and as a means of communication. In Appendix A, you will find a "Progress Memo" that students may use to communicate about their progress, including questions and problems that come up as they move through the project. There is also a "Letter of Evaluation" that students may use at the end of the project to assess their thoughts about the project and their performance. Students are often comfortable with worksheets, and they can be used to create a focused activity when students are at varying places in their project.

Quick Tips for Project Design

- When developing a project, present students with an obvious hook: music, art, sports, and so on.
- If students are resistant when presented with a project idea, reverse the process and do an "into" assignment first to get them involved.
- Combine academic and technical classes for a hands-on project.
- Use the student-developed assessment tools as a way to help students clarify what is expected of them.
- Explore the school resources—PowerPoint software, television studio, choir room—to enhance the project.
- Develop a project organizational system that is simple for you and your students and that includes a template for student instructions as well as a calendar.
- Design worksheets that reinforce skills, provide project instructions, and allow for a written dialogue between students and teacher.
- Allow the project to evolve as you receive feedback from your students.
- Make the culminating activity an "event" to share with other classes.

3

Standards, SCANS, and High-Stakes Testing

Standards and Projects

Projects encompass the complex ideas and very specific skills outlined by the National Council of Teachers of English (NCTE) and the International Reading Association (IRA) in the standards they sponsor (n.d.; see www.ncte.org). The benchmark English/Language Arts skills—reading, writing, speaking, and listening—and the complex tasks of completing a long-term research project allow students significant time to practice and apply standards. Building the components of a portfolio require that students develop a research path based on a thesis supported by a variety of text sources and graphics. Research provides the added value of helping students see how subject matter may be connected. In addition, students utilize their sophisticated understanding of technology and their artistic or dramatic talents to enhance culminating activities when addressing audiences about their research discoveries.

The standards sponsored by NCTE and IRA are straightforward, and at the same time, like all standards, they necessitate that both teachers and students are actively involved in meeting them. It is assumed that teachers will aggressively pursue effective instructional strategies and will receive support from their school site and professional conferences. While there is nothing disingenuous about these hopes, they overlook a careful analysis of our clients—the students. Who they are? How do they learn? What will they need to know and be able to do to function in the adult world? A curious phenomenon of the education world is that we actually know a great deal about how human beings learn and can articulate the needs of students over the lunch table. Despite these conversations, the number of students sitting in high school classrooms misbehaving or professing boredom is an indication that we need to listen to them.

The SCANS Report (Secretary's Commission on Achieving Necessary Skills, 2006) lays out the kinds of skills students must have for the workplace. Among others, these include teamwork, problem solving, social interaction, and acquiring and organizing information. On the surface, these ideas may seem of little value to the English/Language Arts classroom, but they are human behaviors (or skills), characteristics of learning that can be fostered and applied in any "student-centered" classroom, and certainly can be practiced during the development of a literature project.

It is interesting to examine NCTE/IRA Standard 11, which states, "Students participate as knowledgeable, reflective, creative, and critical members of a variety of literacy communities" (see www.ncte .org). It is difficult to understand exactly what is meant by "literacy communities." Perhaps one such literacy community is an English/Language Arts classroom of involved and active students. The remainder of the standard describes the ideal student who understands the basics of being a "successful" student through knowledge, reflection, and creativity. These descriptors create a picture of that lifelong learner so often mentioned in mission statements and posted in school offices. Ironically, students rarely gain the self-awareness that they have the potential to be this person.

Certainly, there are many students who learn in a variety of environments and need little training in how to be a student. And of course, there are just as many, if not more students, who need the opportunity to discover what it means to be successful. The teacher's job is to encourage student confidence, patience, and persistence and provide the opportunities for students to experience success. A student-centered, project-based classroom is meant to bring students to the awareness of their potential, something that never can be reached through expedience or one-size-fits-all learning environments.

Students will not meet standards by enduring punishing classroom environments on a daily basis. Good teaching channels student energy through interesting challenges. The classroom should be less about rules and more about the civility that nurtures student self-awareness.

The habits and expectations of a traditional classroom are so ingrained in both teacher and students that the task of changing course is huge. Think of the miscue students are given concerning grades—"I don't get good grades; therefore, I am not smart." By understanding and developing the criteria for evaluating an assignment, a student has a sense of control over the evaluation process and becomes very familiar with the assignment. Students buried in failure, who procrastinate, use their time poorly, or who disrupt class are offered a productive role in a student-centered classroom. Leading a discussion and peer teaching both require preparation (a distinctly different activity from completing nightly homework) and personal risk involving peers. This active participation is empowering.

Standards for the English Language Arts, Developed by NCTE and IRA

The following list is from the *Standards for the English Language Arts,* by the International Reading Association and the National Council of Teachers of English, copyright 1996 by the International Reading Association and the National Council of Teachers of English. Reprinted with permission. http://www.ncte.org/about/over/standards/110846.htm

- Students read a wide range of print and nonprint texts to build an understanding of texts, of themselves, and of the cultures of the United States and the world; to acquire new information; to respond to the needs and demands of society and the workplace; and for personal fulfillment. Among these texts are fiction and nonfiction, classic and contemporary works.

- Students read a wide range of literature from many periods in many genres to build an understanding of the many dimensions (e.g., philosophical, ethical, aesthetic) of human experience.

- Students apply a wide range of strategies to comprehend, interpret, evaluate, and appreciate texts. They draw on their prior experience, interactions with other readers and writers, their knowledge of word meaning and of other texts, word identification strategies, and their understanding of textual features (e.g., sound-letter correspondence, sentence structure, context, graphics).

- Students adjust their use of spoken, written, and visual language (e.g., conventions, style, vocabulary) to communicate effectively with a variety of audiences and for different purposes.

- Students employ a wide range of strategies as they write and use different writing process elements appropriately to communicate with different audiences for a variety of purposes.

- Students apply knowledge of language structure, language conventions (e.g., spelling and punctuation), media techniques, figurative language and genre to create critique and discuss print and nonprint texts.

- Students conduct research on issues and interests by generating ideas and questions, and by posing problems. They gather, evaluate, and synthesize data from a variety of sources (e.g., print and nonprint texts, artifacts, people) to communicate their discoveries in ways that suit their purpose and audience.

- Students use a variety of technological and information resources (e.g., libraries, databases, computer networks, video) to gather and synthesize information and to create and communicate knowledge.

- Students develop an understanding of and respect for diversity in language use, patterns, and dialects across cultures, ethnic groups, geographic regions, and social roles.

- Students whose first language is not English make use of their first language to develop competency in the English language arts and to develop understanding of content across the curriculum.

- Students participate as knowledgeable, reflective, creative, and critical members of a variety of literacy communities.

- Students use spoken, written, and visual language to accomplish their own purposes (e.g., for learning, enjoyment, persuasion, and the exchange of information).

High-Stakes Testing

Without addressing the pros and cons of high-stakes testing, a student-centered, project-based instructional approach provides students and their teacher the latitude to return to the practice and application of skills covered on standardized tests, while concurrently working to complete a quality project. Because students are aware of the criteria to attain mastery on a project (they develop the criteria or rubric), they want to understand such technicalities as punctuation and citing of sources to do well on their project.

Project-based learning allows for embedded skill practice and the recursive process of revisiting skills and their application in order to master them. During a project, students will request skill review so that they can accurately apply these skills to the text of their projects. Students are also given a tremendous amount of instruction on how to read, analyze, and quote literature through the use of reading and dialectical journals and preparation for discussions. Since projects are based upon reading, students are exposed to a variety of texts and are required to read extensively. The writing process is also emphasized—from brainstorming through revision and research—as the connective thread that runs throughout the project. The intensity and practice of these skills support preparation for standardized testing.

4

Adopt a Poet

Let us go and talk to the poets.

—Joaquin Miller
(the "poet of the Sierras,"
on arriving in San Francisco)

Teacher Instructions

To know and love a poet opens the door to the discovery of many wonderful poets, and yet, high school students do not often get a chance to study poetry in depth. Their typical response to a poetry unit is passionate—they love it or hate it. Above all else, poetry is a mystery to them. They assert that poetry is difficult to understand, and that it must rhyme or sound like a Hallmark greeting card. Those who love it, often use it to express teen angst—especially the perennial broken heart.

To help students become involved in poetry, I ask them to adopt a poet and immerse themselves in the writer's poetry and life. Students synthesize their research thematically, moving away from a straight biographical report to an analysis of the poet's work to produce a formal written analysis of a particular poem, a well-designed poster board, and an oral presentation.

Choosing a Poet and a Poem

Students focus on American, British, or world poets in school. You can do the following to get them started.

- Provide a list of poets.
- Ask students to examine poets in their textbook or sample textbooks you may have in your classroom.
- Ask students to begin with a single poem they enjoy and then move to a collection of poems by the same poet.
- Suggest a thematic search: nature poets; poets who respond to city or rural life; poetry about work, sports, animals, inner psychology, or spirituality.
- Show videotapes of poets reading their work.
- Make several class trips to the school library.
- Ask the school librarian to display poetry books and provide suitable Internet sites for exploration.

Watch out for the following student choices:

- A poet whose poems are commercial or just plain bad (most students will not know the difference)
- A younger poet in the textbook who does not have a sufficient body of work or biographical information
- Too many students focused on popular poets (Poe or Frost)
- A rock musician

Invariably, a few students will have trouble picking a poet. If they become frustrated, give them a weekend to search a bookstore, a local library, the Internet, or their parents' bookshelves, and then help them make the choice; otherwise, they will fall behind.

Promoting Student-Centered Behaviors

Practicing student-centered behaviors is an integral part of the project. Do not separate it from academics. Behavior goes hand in hand with academic success. Throughout the project, students teach punctuation, lead discussions, and help develop the criteria for evaluating writing, presentations, and graphics. When students revert to teacher dependence, stop and refocus them. Guide them by making them aware that they are working toward independent learning and collaboration with other students.

Set aside a bulletin board where students can post library hours, Web sites, and research questions another student may be able to answer.

Embedded Mini Lessons

Embedded mini lessons are "need-to-know" skills students confront as they move through the project, including punctuation, grammar, and endnotes.

Keeping a Calendar

Before you begin this project, block out a tentative calendar noting holidays, assemblies, and other interruptions. You will get a sense where to embed mini lessons and student-led discussions and when students may have time to develop criteria or rubrics.

Once you have explained the project to your students, provide them with a blank calendar. As they move through the project, they will keep a daily record of what they have accomplished. Discuss tasks and due dates with your students so that everyone understands what is expected. Students will provide good feedback and the consensus of the class will be reasonable. On Mondays, before the class begins to work, agree upon what assignments will be completed during the week. On Fridays, develop a weekend plan to accomplish tasks outside of the classroom.

Keep a stack of blank calendars available for students to use (see "Blank Calendar" in Appendix A).

Getting Started

Students complete three products: a graphic representation of the poet's work and life, an essay, and a presentation. Research for all three of these assignments goes on simultaneously, and it is a good idea for students to keep a reading journal to compile their information.

The Research

Biographical information. Biographical information provides a window into the life of a poet, and students soon learn that writers face the same life challenges as the rest of us. Once students gain a general understanding of their poet's life, encourage them to focus on a life experience or philosophy that guides their poet's writing. Perhaps the poet was influenced by politics, foreign travel, other writers, or worked in a factory or on a farm.

Students should use at least three sources (only one of which should be the Internet) and, depending on their ability, should read a biography and a collection of the poet's work.

Choosing a poem. Over the course of their research, students choose a poem that is representative of their poet's work. They write a paper analyzing the poem, use the poem on the poster board, and memorize it for the presentation.

Remind students to begin memorizing their poem as they research, so they will be prepared for their presentation. They should memorize at least 10 to 15 lines; if the poet writes short poems, they may memorize two of them.

The writer on writing. For their poster board, students find a quote by the poet that comments on writing or the writer's life. They may substitute a line from a friend of the poet or a critic if they wish.

If students are researching a living poet, they may be able to use a line from an interview.

The quote is arranged on the poster board as a thematic center-piece or as an interesting fact that adds to the graphic representation of the poet.

Concrete poetry. This is another approach to analysis and a fun one. Students arrange words or lines of the poem on the poster board to create a visual image and to understand the structure of the poem.

Picture of the poet. A photograph or artist's rendering of the poet is included on the poster board.

Poet's name. Students write the poet's name in large letters in the lower right-hand corner of the poster board. This produces an interesting continuity when posters are displayed across the classroom walls.

Annotated bibliography (typed). Students develop an annotated bibliography to document sources and illustrate their relevancy. This is to be typed.

The Written Analysis

Once students have read at least one collection of poetry, they are ready to begin a written analysis of the poem they have chosen to represent the poet's writing. Discuss sample student essays and focus on the development of a thesis. Students often find "quick writes" to be a good way to discover their ideas about the poem, and they can insert parts of this commentary in their essay if it is appropriate.

During the writing phase, ask students to save rewrites of their thesis, quick writes, and any other strategies they may have used to develop a draft of their essay. Copy some of this writing onto overheads and ask students to teach a series of mini lessons on approaches to getting what they want to say on paper. These lessons illustrate the challenge of writing and emphasize writing as a process.

This is also a good time for the class to build a list of criteria (and possibly a rubric) to evaluate the essays.

The essays are to be typed and evaluated by classmates using the criteria or rubric they have developed. When the papers arrive on your desk for a grade, use the same criteria that the class has developed as an evaluation tool.

The Graphic

The poster board is intended to be a graphic synthesis of a student's research. It should reflect an aspect of the poet's life and attitudes about writing. Student poster board projects are often a haphazard collage of pictures and words. For students to get a sense of design or a feeling of what it means to produce a quality product, I usually complete a sample poster board for them. While this is time consuming, it will save you time in the long run if students can see what you are after. When I completed a poster board, a student commented, "Oh, you want a work of art!" I am certainly not an artist, and I assure students they do not have to be either to create a well-designed poster board.

Students should use biographical information, a quote by the writer on writing, a short excerpt from their essay, a picture of the poet, and concrete poetry in their graphic design. The poet's name is placed in the bottom right-hand corner.

Here are some design suggestions to help your students:

- Overlap images, blending or weaving written material with graphics.
- Biographical material and written analysis are best presented as an integral part of the design, rather than typed up. Written material makes a good border, or can be broken up into incremental pieces and repeated.
- Coil tissue paper and aluminum foil to make a colorful raised background.
- Create three-dimensional figures or symbols.
- Design a pop-up feature and attach it to the top of the poster board. (This can be used during the presentation.)
- To narrow the focus, students can use a thematic approach or work within the context of one important event in the poet's life.
- Images need to fill the poster board, rather than drowning in large white spaces.
- Discourage students from typing a list of facts to glue on the poster board.
- Invite an art teacher or art student to speak to your classes about the elements of design.

Presentation

Students share what they have learned about their poet and gain exposure to other poets through student presentations. Presentations are 3 to 5 minutes in length and include a recitation of the poem from memory. As students listen to the presentations, they evaluate them using student-developed criteria or a rubric. A short evaluation form helps students respond quickly and easily to the presentations. Leave a small space at the bottom of the form for a comment. After the presentations are over, students spread their evaluations out on a table so that they are available to the presenters. Leave them there for several days so that students can read them at their leisure.

Tips to Help Students With Presentations

Students should

- Practice their presentation,
- Cut out extraneous information,
- Memorize their poem thoroughly,
- Use biographical material sparingly,
- Use the poster board as a prop (optional).

As the teacher, you should

- Videotape presentations,
- Arrange for students to share presentations in other English classes.

Letter of Evaluation

Each student writes a letter of evaluation addressed to you, reflecting on the quality of their study habits and assignments for this project. Their ideas are supported by quotes from their written work and references to examples they have collected from other sources. The letter also covers use of time management and organization, the challenges of research, how and when the student asked for help and from whom, and what they would do differently if they were to complete another research project (see "Letter of Evaluation" worksheet in Appendix A).

Student Instructions

This research project is designed to help you understand and appreciate poetry. You will choose a poet to read and study and will be required to analyze a poem, write an essay, and design a graphic representation of what you have learned about the poet.

Choose a Poet

To select a poet, begin your search in the classroom. Browse through your textbook and any material your teacher may provide. Look on the bookshelves at home and visit the school library. You may find you have an interest in common with a poet, or you may enjoy a poet's writing because it is playful. Check to make sure you can find plenty of background material on the poet of your choice. Some living poets may be too young to have much written about them. Keep an alternative poet in mind.

Try broadening your knowledge of poets. Many of you enjoy Edgar Allan Poe and Robert Frost, but there are many interesting poets and you will benefit from reading a poet who is new to you.

Pick a Poem

Select a poem from a collection of the poet's work to use as the focus of your project. You will analyze this poem in an essay, integrate it into a poster board graphic, and memorize it, so choose carefully. You will want to pick a poem with enough substance to utilize it in a variety of ways.

Biographical Information and Influences of People and the Times

Use at least three different sources to find biographical information about the poet. Discover what friends, colleagues, and critics say about the poet's work. If the poet is still alive, what does the person say about him- or herself? Did cultural ideas or historical events influence the poet's writing?

Quote Your Poet

Note comments the poet makes about world events, writing, friends, and family. When you are ready to complete your poster board, choose a quote by your poet that supports a theme or idea you represent on your poster board.

Concrete Poetry

Concrete poetry is a playful method of expressing subject and form. Play with your poet's poem using symbols and images and use your poster board to express these. Use this creative approach to the poem as part of the design of your poster board. You can find examples of concrete poetry on the Internet. (See "Sample of Concrete Poetry" in Appendix B.)

Picture of the Poet

Find a photograph or drawing of your poet. Photocopy or scan it and add it to your poster. Make sure it fits into the overall design.

The Written Analysis

In an essay, analyze the poem you chose to represent your poet's work. Your teachers and classmates will help you with your writing. Here are some suggestions for getting started: Read the poem and jot down your personal response. Instead of reading to the end of a line, read to the end of a sentence to understand what your poet is saying. You may use "I" when talking about your impressions of the poem. Write in your voice rather than trying to sound scholarly. Support your ideas with selected lines from the poem.

To understand what characteristics you are aiming for in this paper, your class, with the help of your teacher, will make a list of criteria. Use the criteria as a guide to help you write well. The final draft of your essay will be typed.

The Graphic

When thinking about a design for your poster board, consider your research, topics of interest to your poet, and the poem you have chosen to represent the poet's writing. Complete a preliminary sketch of your poster board design. Think of your poster board as a graphic map of your oral presentation. What graphic features will help you when you give your presentation?

From Your Research

Listed below are elements from researching and thinking about your poet to use on your poster board.

- Lines from the poem (you may use your concrete poem for this)
- A quote on writing from your poet (or a quote about the poet's writing from another source)
- Several lines from your essay (if appropriate)
- A picture of the poet
- Carefully selected biographical information
- The poet's name written boldly in the bottom right-hand corner

Ideas for a Beautiful Graphic

- Overlap images, blending or weaving written material with the graphics.
- Present biographical material and written analysis as an integral part of the design, rather than typed. Written material makes a good border, or can be broken up into incremental pieces so that it is easily communicated.
- Coil tissue paper and aluminum foil to make a colorful raised background.
- Create three-dimensional figures or symbols.
- Design a pop-up graphic that is attached to the top of the poster board.
- Focus on a theme or one idea.
- Fill the entire poster board—do not let images drown in white space.
- Do not list facts; integrate them into the overall design.
- Discuss your ideas with an art teacher or a friend in an art class.

Annotated Bibliography

Please develop an annotated bibliography documenting your sources. This should be typed. Attach it to the back of your poster board.

Presentation

Share your expertise about the poet with your classmates. Develop a presentation that will help your classmates learn about the poet you chose to research. Your presentation will be 3 to 5 minutes in length and will include a recitation of the poem you have memorized.

Here are some suggestions for developing a good presentation:

- Keep your presentation within the time limit.
- Practice in front of family and friends.
- Recite the poem, then provide analysis, relevant biographical information (don't give your poet's entire life story), and the poet's thoughts on writing.
- Integrate your poster board into your presentation.
- If you feel you could improve the presentation by doing it over, arrange to present it to another class.

5

Project Monster

The stories are mostly about people and not monsters.

—Stephen King

Teacher Instructions

This project was inspired by a class of seniors who were more than a little reluctant to study British literature. Since they happily read a wide variety of contemporary "horror" novels and loved to be scared out of their wits watching frightening movies, using some of the more famous literary monsters seemed a good way of introducing British literature.

Older students do justice to this project by mastering the reading and doing some substantive research, although the project has been modified over the years for younger students. Students research a monster from literature, an abstract monster (from medicine, society, science, history, or psychology), or a generic monster: a witch, werewolf, or vampire. Based upon a thorough reading of relevant literature and extensive research, students utilize language arts skills to produce a portfolio, an essay, and a presentation.

Literary Monsters

This project was originally designed for seniors who were not enthused about studying British literature. Since they usually read one classic featuring a monster, I thought perhaps a focus on monsters would interest them. *Beowulf, Frankenstein, Dracula,* and *The*

Strange Case of Dr. Jekyll and Mr. Hyde are novels that combine monsters and literature and make for interesting research projects. The play *The Crucible* and an examination of witches can lead to an exploration of historical witch hunts. For strong readers, *Mary Reilly* is the perfect companion to *Dr. Jekyll and Mr. Hyde*, as is *Grendel* to *Beowulf* and *Wicked* to *The Wonderful Wizard of Oz*.

Abstract Monsters

A spin-off from the literary monster is the abstract monster. Students research a topic that challenges the human experience, is manifested by human behavior individually or collectively, or stems from the natural world. Poverty, disease, racism, and weather-related monsters are a few of the abstract monsters that interest students. One senior even examined romantic love as a monster.

Researching an abstract monster provides students with skills beyond the usual literary analysis and prepares them for college research. These students may visit a college library to read professional journals and contact organizations that specialize in health or science issues. For example, if a student is studying AIDS, he or she has the option to contact the World Health Organization, the Centers for Disease Control, or the United Nations.

There is also a strong literary basis for abstract monsters. In Poe's short stories, alone, one can find many human emotions and experiences that could be studied as monsters. Here is a sampling: "The Telltale Heart" (guilt as monster), "The Black Cat" (man as monster), and "The Masque of the Red Death" (plague as monster). Another powerful example of a monster is Shirley Jackson's famous short story, "The Lottery," which reveals the "system" as a monster.

Although students usually have no trouble adapting this project to explore an abstract monster, some assignments work better than others and students can choose among them. You may have some valuable suggestions as well. It is the discussion between teacher and student that really brings worthwhile ideas into focus.

Generic Monsters

Younger students tend to gravitate toward a type of monster to research such as werewolves, dragons, or witches. They are often surprised to discover entire books on their monster as well as connections to superstition, film, children's stories, and annual traditions such as Halloween. Where advanced students may start with literature, younger students stumble on it when they discover myths, poems, short stories, and children's stories featuring their monster.

To modify this unit, assess the skills and interests of your students and choose appropriate assignments from the list. Students do not need to complete the entire portfolio. Typically, they are interested in art, music, and children's literature, and enjoy writing poetry. Depending on the students, they may choose to skip the essay in favor of polishing their presentation. If time allows, offer them a second chance to present. They are often willing to perfect their presentations, paying close attention to the criteria the class has developed.

Introducing Students to Monsters

As an introductory activity, show brief clips of horror movies. Isolate particular scenes. Five minutes of an old black-and-white Dracula movie will have them in stitches, bore them, or incite an interest in vampires.

To promote reading, set up a book table displaying classic horror stories (or ask the school librarian to do this). Reading book jackets will help students to discover an interest—and an appropriate reading level. And no, they cannot read Stephen King. The point of the project is to read a classic. (Although in their research, they might quote him or other contemporary writers of the horror genre.)

Book Contract

After brainstorming a list of monsters and reviewing project requirements together as a class, students spend time in the library browsing and using the Internet. Many of them will identify a monster and narrow their topic quickly. At this stage, they are ready to complete a book contract (see "Book Contract" in Appendix C). A small number of students will have trouble choosing a topic. Help them narrow their topic and give them a time limit.

Keeping a Calendar

Before you begin this project, block out a tentative calendar noting holidays, assemblies, and other interruptions. This will help you get a sense of where to embed mini lessons and student-led discussions, and when students may have time to develop criteria or rubrics.

Once you have explained the project to your students, provide them with a blank calendar (see Appendix A). As they move through the project, they will keep a daily record of what they have accomplished. Discuss tasks and due dates with your students so that everyone understands what is expected. Students will provide good feedback and the consensus of the class will be reasonable. On Mondays, before the class begins to work, agree upon what assignments will be completed during the week. On Fridays, develop a weekend plan to accomplish tasks outside of the classroom.

Keep a stack of blank calendars available for students to use.

Research Assignments

Section I: The Monster

Students choose at least one assignment from each section of the project. Many individual assignments potentially could become research projects in and of themselves. Overall, students are exposed to a variety of ideas and creative approaches. An assignment of particular interest to a student may also result in an interesting thesis for an essay.

Introduce Your Monster

The purpose of this assignment is to introduce a variety of monsters to the class. After students read and research their monster, they write an "I Am the One Who" poem or a "found" poem (see student instructions for these in the Appendix C).

Advanced students may feel this assignment is too elementary. If they wish, they can introduce their monster by selecting a descriptive passage from the literature and analyzing the monster's significant characteristics.

Students read their poem or descriptive passage (with analysis) to the class to introduce their monster.

Note: Abstract monsters have identifiable characteristics that can be described.

Section 2: Analysis

Become Your Monster's Psychiatrist

In this assignment, students put their monster on the psychiatrist's couch. Through this interview process, they analyze the monster's passions and needs. The purpose of this assignment is to help students understand the role the monster plays in literature and how an abstract monster impacts human life. Students type up their interview.

The Monster as a Representation of the Human Psyche

Students consider whether their monster reflects an aspect of the human psyche, what psychological truths the monster reveals about human beings or human culture, and whether their monster embodies a scientific or political idea. Using current news stories, they examine how human beings cope with this monster. If they are using an abstract monster, they may also consider how human beings perceive disease, emotions, death, and the advancement of medical research and whether these monsters remind humans of their fragility or mortality. Students choose to write an essay, interview, letter, or several news articles. Students format their work and type it.

Section 3: More Analysis

A Comparison of the Monster and the Protagonist in Literature

Students compare and contrast the monster to the protagonist in the literature selection. For example, in *The Hobbit,* both Bilbo and Gollum are determined and clever; however, the obvious difference is that one represents good and the other evil. Encourage students to look for subtle comparisons as well, and then ask them to develop a graphic organizer that illustrates what they have discovered. They will need to use quotes to support their ideas.

Graphic organizers may include sequential boxes, a Venn diagram, or large outlines of the characters filled with information. Quotes are inserted inside the graphic organizer, at the bottom, or around the edges. Allow students to develop the graphic, but insist on neatness.

The Monster's Side of the Story: A Monologue

Students write a monologue from the monster's perspective, allowing it to explain its side of a particular conflict. The monster howls and whines, showing its fury and sorrow. Remind students that abstract monsters can speak as well.

Battles

Students illustrate a physical battle or analyze a battle of wits between the monster and its enemy and provide an explanation of what is occurring. If students are using an abstract monster, they can consider how disease battles the immune system, how poverty or abuse battles the physical or mental well-being of a person, or how political ideas and scientific research encounter opposition.

Section 4: Making Other Connections

Monsters in Children's Literature

In this assignment, students compare a monster in children's fiction with the monster they are studying. They explore fairy tales, nursery rhymes, and other children's stories to learn how monsters are depicted and examine plot, theme, and life lessons manifested. They may use a Venn diagram (with commentary below it) or a written explanation to make a comparison.

Note: This assignment may not work for abstract monsters, although students often come up with interesting ideas to modify it.

Monsters in Art

Students research monsters in art and film to examine their visual impact. For example, what kinds of images evoke fear, reflection, or laughter? How does film create a frightening monster (or a silly monster)? What powerful images of monsters can be found in paintings? Are the visual images of monsters in comic books simply meant to represent evil, or do they have another function?

Students photocopy sample paintings, drawings, and movie posters and write commentary beneath their examples.

Monsters in Music

Students research "monster music" from any genre—folk, classical, opera, or contemporary song—to find a musical expression of the monster. They may be unable to find the monster they are studying, but it is useful for them to explore music for a monster connection. They will consider the following questions, among others: Does the music impart an emotional understanding of the monster? What inspired the creation of the composition? Are there important cultural connections related to the music? Who listens or listened to the music? If the music has lyrics, how would you describe them?

Students provide a written analysis of the music, typing up the lyrics (if the music has them) and including interesting background information. To enhance this assignment, they may provide a tape of the music or a photocopy of the CD jacket cover.

Note: Abstract monsters may be of the emotional variety: revenge, love lost, or jealousy.

Symbol Dictionary

Students create a symbol dictionary using words and graphics to explain objects, ideas, and places that have special meaning to their monster. For example, they may use symbols or drawings to represent greed, fire, gold, caves, forests, animals, garlic, and so forth. Encourage them to look for universal symbols before creating their own representation. Their dictionaries will be more interesting if they draw the symbols rather than using clip art.

Their dictionary will resemble an illustrated children's dictionary. Next to each symbol or drawing, students explain how it relates to the monster's passion. They may handwrite or type their dictionary.

Note: Abstract monsters may be associated with medical, scientific, and political symbols.

Origin of Monster

Students develop a family tree, graphic organizer, or drawing, with handwritten or typed explanations of their monster's origin. They consider whether their monster is found in history, oral tradition, or myth, and whether it is a monster born to parents or created by human beings in literature or superstition.

Note: An abstract monster might begin life as a cell mutation, a miscommunication, or a political or economic condition.

Compiling the Portfolio

If students or classes are not writing an essay, they can begin to assemble their portfolio. Emphasize organization and neatness, and provide students with the format for their cover page and table of contents.

Section 5: Essay

Students choose an essay topic by reviewing the literature and project assignments, and by reading journal entries. Encourage them to pick a topic of personal interest and a thesis that they can support. Since they will have gathered a considerable amount of information, you may need to help them narrow their topic and develop a workable thesis.

Portfolio

A portfolio is an organizational tool and a showcase for the student project. All work is typed and examples are photocopied, illustrated, and labeled. The format is formal and should meet your specifications. Neatness counts! As the class develops criteria for evaluating portfolios, discuss what it means to complete quality work.

The portfolio includes the following pieces:

Cover page (typed)
Provide format.

Table of Contents (typed)

Letter of Evaluation
Each student writes a letter of evaluation addressed to you, reflecting on the quality of their study habits and project assignments. Their ideas should be supported by quotes from their written work and

references to examples they have collected from other sources. The letter also covers their use of time management and organization, the challenges of research, how and when the student asked for help and from whom, and what they would do differently if they were to complete another research project (see questions for "Letter of Evaluation" in Appendix A).

Essay

Project Monster Assignments

Annotated Bibliography (typed)

Students develop an annotated bibliography to document sources and illustrate their relevancy. This should be typed.

A Reading Journal

Each student keeps a reading journal to take notes; explore ideas; and record page numbers, quotations, and document sources. A reading journal authenticates the reading completed by students and is handwritten. It is placed at the back of the portfolio.

Calendar

Handwritten Annotations

On the day the project is due, students review their work and make handwritten comments on the pages of their project (they may use Post-its). They are often reluctant to write on their beautifully typed packet, but through review, they will discover new insights about their research. Often their informal comments reflect a surprising understanding of the subject.

Presentation

Students share what they have learned with the class by creating a 3- to 5-minute presentation. They use assignments from their portfolio to develop an interesting idea, and clarify it by filling out a presentation worksheet (see sample in Appendix C). Here are a few ideas students have used:

Introduction

- Recite a poem describing the monster.
- Use an important statement by the monster.
- Play a brief musical selection.
- Display a graphic or work of art.

Body of Presentation

- Introduce a thesis and support it with facts and ideas.
- Explain a battle and the outcome.
- Compare an artist's conception of the monster with an author's description.
- Provide background information about a contemporary abstract monster and discuss strategies for solving this issue.
- Present a dramatic monologue from the monster's point of view.
- Compare and contrast the monster and the protagonist or create a dialogue between them (see "Presentation Worksheet" in Appendix C).

Student Instructions

You have heard of Dracula and Frankenstein's monster, but who exactly are they? Why are they so famous? In this project, you will choose a monster to research, complete a variety of creative projects, and then share your knowledge with the class.

Monsters in Literature

Research a monster in literature by reading a novel or a combination of essays, poems, myths, and short stories. Here are a few famous classics: *Dracula, Frankenstein, The Strange Case of Dr. Jekyll and Mr. Hyde,* and *Beowulf.* If you want a challenge, try reading two companion novels such as *Dr. Jekyll and Mr. Hyde* and *Mary Reilly,* or *Beowulf* and *Grendel.*

Abstract Monsters

Once you start thinking about abstract monsters, you will find them everywhere. They include human emotions (hatred, jealousy), disease (AIDS, Ebola virus, SARS), historical phenomena (war, torture, dictatorship), and environmental disasters (hurricanes, earthquakes, pollution). Try brainstorming a list of them with your classmates.

If you choose an abstract monster, you may want to visit a college library, which will have medical and scientific journals as well as extensive information on history, psychology, and other topics. You may also use the Internet and newspapers, as they are good sources of articles on current, newsworthy subjects.

Even though you may read a great deal of factual information, some topics lend themselves to literature as well. Here is a starting point for monsters dealing with human emotions in short stories:

Edgar Allan Poe's "The Black Cat" (man as monster), "The Masque of the Red Death" (plague as monster), and "The Telltale Heart" (guilt as monster). Shirley Jackson's short story "The Lottery" is a good place to begin studying "the system" as monster.

Generic Monsters

Witches, werewolves, vampires, and dragons are all monsters you can research. Not only will you find information about them, you will also find they figure in legends, fairy tales, and children's stories.

Please fill out a Book Contract when you have chosen your topic. Your reading list may grow, but it is important to make a commitment to a monster and begin your research.

Calendar

Once you understand the requirements for this project, use a calendar (provided by your teacher) to note assignment due dates. You will discuss assignments and due dates weekly with your teacher. You will also decide what homework you need to complete for the weekend. Place this calendar behind your reading journal in your portfolio. There is no need to type it.

Research Assignments

Below, you will find a list of assignments to help you understand a monster. Please pick at least one assignment from each section. Note: If you are researching an abstract monster, you may have to modify the assignments. Use the suggestions for abstract monsters listed under each assignment or develop your own. When you have completed these assignments, organize them in your portfolio.

Section 1: Introduce Your Monster

To introduce your monster to the class, write an "I Am the One Who" poem or a "found" poem describing the monster. Your teacher will provide you with instructions on how to write these poems. Or, introduce the monster by selecting a descriptive passage from the literature and analyzing the monster's significant characteristics. Read your poem or descriptive passage with analysis to the class.

Note: There is no need to modify this assignment if you have chosen an abstract monster. After all, monsters express themselves in one form or another. Think about the monster and its identifiable characteristics. How is AIDS described by a scientist or doctor? How does a soldier, philosopher, or journalist describe war? How is jealousy or any other human emotion described by a psychologist? How does a meteorologist describe a hurricane or a tsunami?

Section 2: Analysis

Become Your Monster's Psychiatrist

In this assignment, you will become the monster's psychiatrist. Let the monster lie on the psychiatrist's couch while you analyze its passions and needs. Develop an interview between the psychiatrist (you) and the monster.

Political and social issues, weather, emotions, and other abstract monsters can lie down on the psychiatrist's couch to explore a need to destroy or transform.

Please type your final draft in interview or essay form.

Your Monster as a Representation of the Human Psyche

Write a brief essay addressing one of the following questions: Does your monster reflect an aspect of the human psyche? What psychological truths does your monster reveal about human beings or human culture? Does your monster embody a scientific or political idea? If so, what? Can you find any contemporary news articles that reflect an aspect of your monster? How do human beings cope with this monster? (Be sure to support your ideas.)

Choose a format that best fits your ideas. Consider writing an essay, interview, letter, or several news articles. Format your work accordingly and type the final draft.

Section 3: More Analysis

Comparing Your Monster and the Protagonist in Literature

Compare and contrast your monster to the protagonist in the literature selection. For example, in *The Hobbit*, both Bilbo and Gollum are determined and clever; however, the obvious difference is that one represents good and the other evil. Look for subtle comparisons as well, and develop a graphic organizer that illustrates the similarities and differences you discover. Use quotes to support your ideas.

Graphic organizers may include sequential boxes, a Venn diagram, or large outlines of the characters filled with information. Quotes are inserted inside the graphic organizer, at the bottom, or around the edges. You may design your own graphic, but remember, neatness counts!

Your Monster's Side of the Story

Write a monologue from the monster's perspective, allowing it to explain its side of a particular conflict. Let your monster howl and whine to show its fury and sorrow. Remember, abstract monsters can speak, too.

Battles

Illustrate a physical battle or analyze a battle of wits between the monster and its enemy and provide an explanation of what is occurring. If you are using an abstract monster, consider how disease battles the immune system, how poverty or abuse battles the physical or mental well-being of a person, or how political ideas and scientific research encounter opposition.

Section 4: Making Other Connections

Monsters in Children's Literature

In this assignment, you will compare a monster in children's fiction with the monster you are studying. Explore fairy tales, nursery rhymes, and other children's stories to learn how monsters are depicted. Examine plot, theme, and life lessons manifested in these stories. Collect your ideas and use a Venn diagram (with commentary below it) or a written explanation to make a comparison.

Your Monster in Art

Research monsters in art and film to examine their visual impact. For example, what kinds of images evoke fear, reflection, or laughter? How does film create a frightening monster (or a silly monster)? What powerful images of monsters can be found in paintings? Are the visual images of monsters in comic books simply meant to represent evil, or do they have another function?

Photocopy sample paintings, drawings, and movie posters, and write commentary beneath your examples.

Note: For an abstract monster, show how your monster is depicted graphically in science books, or how an artist or photographer conveys the results of a monster's work—for example, the plague, AIDS, famine, weather.

Your Monster and Music

Research "monster music" from any genre—folk, classical, opera, or contemporary song—to find a musical expression of the monster. You may be unable to find the monster you are studying, but it is interesting to explore "monster" music. Consider the following questions, among others: Does the music impart an emotional understanding of the monster? What inspired the creation of the composition? Are there important cultural connections related to the music? Who listens or listened to the music? If the music has lyrics, how would you describe them?

Provide a written analysis of the music, typing up the lyrics (if the music has them), and include interesting background information. To enhance this assignment, provide a tape of the music or a photocopy of the CD jacket cover.

Note: Abstract monsters may be of the emotional variety: revenge, love lost, or jealousy.

Symbol Dictionary

Create a symbol dictionary using words and graphics to explain objects, ideas, and places that have special meaning to the monster. For example, use symbols or drawings to represent greed, fire, gold, caves, forests, animals, garlic, and so forth. Look for common symbols before creating your own representation. (Your dictionary will be more interesting if you illustrate it rather than using clip art.)

Your dictionary will resemble an illustrated children's dictionary. Beside each symbol or drawing, explain how it relates to your monster's passion. Handwrite or type your dictionary.

Note: Abstract monsters may be associated with medical, scientific, and political symbols.

Origin of Your Monster

Develop a family tree or graphic organizer with handwritten or typed explanations of your monster's origin. Consider whether your monster is found in history, oral tradition, myth, or superstition and whether it had parents or siblings.

Note: An abstract monster might begin life as a cell mutation, a miscommunication, or a political or economic condition.

Section 5: Essay

When choosing a topic for an essay, review the assignments you have completed for this project. Consider the literature you have read and the entries you have made in your reading journal. Pick a topic that interests you and a thesis you will be able to support. You have gathered a considerable amount of information, and it is important that you narrow your topic so that your essay is a manageable one. Work with your teacher and classmates to develop a good thesis.

Portfolio

A portfolio is a showcase for your research project. The presentation of your work is important and should be typed, photocopied, illustrated, photographed, and labeled with care. Organization and neatness count, and you are encouraged to add creative touches as you compile your work.

Your portfolio should include the following elements:

Cover Page
Use your teacher's format.

Table of Contents
A table of contents will help you organize your portfolio.

Letter of Evaluation
Write a letter to your teacher in which you evaluate your portfolio according to the criteria that you have developed with your class. Your letter is the last assignment you will complete before turning in your packet, and your teacher will give you instructions on how to write it. Please insert in your portfolio after the table of contents.

Essay

Research Assignments
Organize your assignments here.

Annotated Bibliography (typed)
An annotated bibliography documents your sources and demonstrates why they are relevant to your topic. Please type.

A Reading Journal
Insert your reading journal in the back of your portfolio. You do not need to type it. Think of it as your notes for the project.

Calendars
Insert the calendars you kept during the project. Don't try to type them.

Handwritten Annotations
On the day the portfolio is due, you will review your work in class and make handwritten comments on the pages (use Post-its if you wish). You may not want to write on your beautifully typed packet, but through review, you will discover new insights. Informal

comments that you make in the margins can help demonstrate the depth of your understanding.

Presentation

The purpose of your presentation is to share what you have learned from your research with the class and possibly other classes. Since you will not be able to share everything you have learned about your monster, review your portfolio to decide what information is important to share. You may give an informational presentation on an abstract monster or a dramatic presentation from a literary monster's perspective.

The Presentation Worksheet needs to be filled out and turned in to your teacher for comments. This will allow your teacher to review the plan for your presentation and help you with any equipment needs. The ideas on the worksheet are not mandatory. Please feel free to come up with your own. Your presentation will be 3 to 5 minutes long. Please practice at home with family and friends before you present to the class.

6

"I Was Friends With . . ."

Some people go to priests; others to poetry; I to my friends.

—Virginia Woolf

Teacher Instructions

This research project requires the student to develop a "friendship" with an author. Students respond to assignments from this perspective and compile their work in a portfolio. They share their understanding of their author with the class by giving a presentation.

Students read a novel, an autobiography or biography, and the author's correspondence with friends and family, and explore historical and artistic trends that influenced the writer's work.

Authors

Virginia Woolf was used in the initial prototype for this project. She had an extensive circle of friends, family, and fellow artists, and she has written journals, letters, and novels for students to explore. There is far more background information available about Woolf than a student needs for this project. For the most part, students are pleasantly surprised by how easily an author's world opens to them. In fact, many a famous author will fall from grace as students discover the human being behind the mystique.

A handful of writers in the literature textbooks will be too young for students to find sufficient background information about them. An author such as J.D. Salinger, who insisted on privacy, will frustrate students, although with the advent of the Internet, they can find a compilation of his work, books written about him, and movies relating to his life.

In the interest of time, encourage students to move quickly from choosing an author to researching. Some students launch into their research and never look back. They arrive in the classroom armed with a novel and research material. A handful of students will have trouble choosing an author and will need help.

Reading

Students are required to read the following:

- At least one novel by the author
- A critical review of the novel
- An autobiography or biography
- Excerpts of journal entries and correspondence
- Relevant historical facts, social and cultural trends, and news articles

Because the reading requirements are demanding, set aside reading days for the students. Students will indicate a need for seatwork, and if you work together to pace the reading and research, they will not become overwhelmed. To manage these days, use calendars to make agreements about time management and due dates. Ask students to assess what they need to accomplish, and then walk around the classroom to monitor progress and help students.

If there are students who respond to seatwork as if it were free time, partner them with another student and develop a peer tutoring agreement. Or, stop students and remind them that time management is an assignment and needs to be practiced with awareness. This conversation will reestablish mutual trust between you and your students. Remember, students like independence, but most of all they want your approval and will work for a compliment.

Reading Journal

Each student keeps a reading journal in which to take notes; explore ideas; and record page numbers, quotations, and document sources. A reading journal authenticates the reading completed by students and is handwritten. It is placed at the back of the portfolio. (See "Reading Journal Instructions" in Appendix A.)

Modifying the Project

To modify this project, students choose an author and read excerpts from a novel, or focus on short stories or poems. They research background information and write a letter from the perspective of a friend of the author's, demonstrating an understanding of the author's writing and life experience. This synthesis of information through writing helps them to clarify what they have learned.

Promoting Student-Centered Behaviors

Practicing student-centered behaviors is an integral part of the project and should not be seen as separate from the academics. Behaviors go hand in hand with academic success. Throughout the project, students teach punctuation; lead discussions; and help develop the criteria for evaluating writing, presentations, and graphics. When students revert to teacher dependence, stop and refocus them. Guide them by making them aware that they are working toward independent learning and collaboration with other students.

Set aside a bulletin board where students can post library hours, helpful Web sites, and research questions another student may be able to answer.

Embedded Mini Lessons

Embedded mini lessons are "need-to-know" skills students confront as they move through the project, including punctuation, grammar, and endnotes.

Keeping a Calendar

Before you begin this project, block out a tentative calendar noting holidays, assemblies, and other interruptions (see "Sample Teacher's Calendar" in Appendix D). You will get a sense of where to embed mini lessons and student-led discussions as well as when students may have time to develop criteria or rubrics.

Once you have explained the project to your students, provide them with a blank calendar. As they move through the project, they will keep a daily record of what they have accomplished. Discuss tasks and due dates with your students so that everyone understands what is expected. The students will provide good feedback and the consensus of the class will be reasonable. On Mondays, before the class begins to work, agree upon what assignments will be completed during the week. On Fridays, develop a weekend plan to accomplish tasks outside of the classroom.

Keep a stack of blank calendars available for students to use (see "Blank Calendar" in Appendix A).

Additional Organization

Save yourself time by providing students with a bulletin board to share research information and a table with extra assignment sheets and reference books.

Research Assignments

Relationship to Author

Students choose their relationship to the author after reading and researching background information. They may select a role other than friend, such as family member, artist, teacher, or journalist. Remind students that they must remain in character throughout the project.

Book Review

Students write a book review on the novel they have read by their author. (Some students may prefer to write an essay.) Provide them with sample book reviews or ask them to find samples to share with the class. Post a review on the student bulletin board so students can refer to it.

Glossary of Terms

Students develop a glossary of words and terms they encounter in researching their author: foreign words; slang; or vocabulary specific to geography, history, art, or food. Each entry must demonstrate the relevance of the word to the author.

Circle of Friends

Students assemble a gallery of photographs (or sketches) of their author's circle of friends and relatives. They include a photograph of themselves. Each person is identified by name, relationship to author, and profession or other personal information.

Impressions of Author's Hometown or Geographical Region

With maps, photographs, and facts, students portray a significant place where the author lived and worked. Using insights from their research and the comments of the author's family and friends, students demonstrate the importance of place (or the lack of it) to their writer. Place may include a region, urban or rural setting, the pleasures of home and garden, or descriptions of place from the writer's work.

Historical Events and Social Trends

Students collect newspaper headlines, famous legal cases, and advertising to provide a context for understanding their writer's response to the social and political issues of the day. Did the writer go to war, protest a political or social issue, or feel the effects of an economic downturn?

Students organize photocopies of the artifacts they find and combine them with commentary to clarify how history affected a writer's life and work.

School libraries generally have a collection of reference books that reflect historical periods and pertinent social trends.

Artistic Ideas

Students research the effects of artistic and literary movements on their author (stream-of-consciousness, realism, cubism, surrealism, etc.) and connect their author to other writers and artists of the period. To reflect the thinking of the times, they use writing samples (of other authors) and display photocopies of sculpture and paintings.

Students organize this collection of work by writers and artists with comments about how this work inspired the author.

Letters to the Author

This section is an imaginary exchange of letters between author and student. Students are required to write at least two letters from the author's point of view and two in response as a friend. Students may use authentic letters written by the author if they are able to respond to their contents. They may photocopy the original letters.

The Interview

The interview is a synthesis of what students have learned about their author. A fictitious journalist or academician poses questions about the author's writing and life and the friend answers the questions. (A student who has chosen an alternative relationship [other than friend] to the author may answer the interview questions from this perspective.) Students develop interview questions and answer them. The interview is to be typed, and may be part of the presentation.

Portfolio

A portfolio is a showcase for a student project, an organizational tool. The format is formal, and all work is typed. Artwork, photographs, and written samples are photocopied or illustrated and labeled. Prior to completing a portfolio, students develop the criteria and a rubric (if time permits) for evaluation purposes.

The portfolio includes the following pieces:

Cover Page (typed)
Provide format.

Table of Contents (typed)

Student Letter of Evaluation (typed)
Each student writes a letter of evaluation addressed to you, reflecting on the quality of his or her study habits and project assignments. Students' ideas are supported by quotes from their written work and references to examples they have collected from other sources. The letter also covers use of time management and organization, the challenges of research, how and when the students asked for help and from whom, and what they would do differently if they were to complete another research project (see questions for "Letter of Evaluation" in Appendix A).

Annotated Bibliography (typed)
Students develop an annotated bibliography to document sources and illustrate their relevancy. This should be typed.

The Reading Journal
The reading journal is handwritten and placed at the back of the portfolio.

Calendar (handwritten)
Before you begin this project, block out a tentative calendar noting holidays, assemblies, and other interruptions. You will get a sense of where to embed mini lessons and student-led discussions as well as when students may have time to develop criteria or rubrics.

Once you have explained the project to your students, provide them with a blank calendar. Refer to it to align your expectations and student needs. Ask students to note what they have accomplished on a daily basis. On Fridays, discuss work for the weekend. Keep a stack of blank calendars available for students to use (see "Sample Teacher's Calendar" in Appendix D).

Handwritten Annotations
On the day the project is due, students review their work and make handwritten comments on the pages of their project (they may use Post-its, if they prefer). They may be reluctant to write on their

beautifully typed packet, but through this review, they will discover new insights about their research. Often these informal comments reflect a surprising understanding of the subject.

This is also a good time for students to share their portfolios with their classmates.

Presentation

Students spend considerable time researching their topic, and they gain the expertise to share what they have learned about their author with the class. Typically, they choose one of the following presentation formats:

- A formal speech about the author from the perspective of a friend
- A dramatic monologue by the friend of the author
- The interview from the portfolio (using another student as interviewer)
- A skit using class members
- The "hot seat" (the class interviews the friend of the author)

Students come up with other creative plans as well. One year, a group of students convinced me they could pull off a "meeting of the minds." Assuming the role of friends, they sat around a table discussing their authors' ideas and jumping back and forth to different time periods. (I would not recommend this particular project for all students. It is rather difficult.)

I don't allow skits to be videotaped at home and shown in the classroom. They are rarely successful and usually very silly. On the other hand, videotaping presentations performed in the classroom is a great way to review and evaluate the presentations. Students love to watch their own presentation.

Set reasonable time limits; otherwise, your presentations will take up too much instructional time. Presentations of 3 to 5 minutes each will work if students have practiced them. A "meeting of the minds" or skit may take longer.

Student presentations are evaluated in terms of mastery, proficiency, or basic skills, and students develop the criteria for each level. There are some students set on achieving mastery, and if they don't reach it on the first try, they will want to present again. I ask them to make an arrangement to present in another classroom. Some students give their presentation over and over and ask administrators to evaluate them as well. Each audience uses the same evaluation criteria to rate the presentations.

Evaluating Student Work

Remember, evaluation is a joint effort between you and your students. With your help, students develop criteria and rubrics to assess portfolios and presentations. These evaluation tools are as important to the process as they are to the product. There is no better way to understand the requirements of a project than to help develop the criteria for evaluating it.

Essays, book reviews, and interviews are among the assignments that are important to grade as students complete them. Don't let yourself get overwhelmed by paperwork at the end of the project.

Student Instructions

During this project, you assume the role of friend to an author. (You may choose an alternative role if you wish.) It is from this perspective that you complete the research assignments and become acquainted with your author's life and writing. You will then compile your work in a portfolio and share your expertise with the class through a presentation.

Calendar

Once you understand the project, use a blank calendar to track your research progress (your teacher will provide this). Note weekly assignments, homework, and due dates on the calendar. Every week, your class will discuss what needs to be accomplished in order to move through the project. When you have completed the project, place this calendar behind your reading journal in your portfolio. The calendar should be handwritten rather than typed.

A Student-Centered Project

This project will allow you to take responsibility for your learning in the classroom. You will lead small- and large-group discussions, peer tutor, develop criteria and rubrics to evaluate your work, and teach skills (punctuation, documentation) to your classmates. In turn, your teacher will give you feedback about your ideas and help you to research and organize your work.

Choosing an Author

Review the list of authors provided by your teacher. Visit the school library and other libraries in your community. Librarians are there to help you—use their expertise.

Your textbook will feature a few contemporary authors. There may or may not be enough background on them for this research project. If you are not sure, ask your teacher. It is a good idea to have an alternate author in mind.

Reading Requirements

Review the list of reading requirements to make sure you understand them. If, after choosing your author, you have questions, please discuss them with your teacher. Use your reading journal to make notes as you read the following:

- At least one novel by your author. As you read, think about these questions: Is there a specific topic or theme your author is particularly fond of exploring? What do you notice about your author's writing style?
- An autobiography or biography to help you understand the events and ideas that shaped your author's life and writing
- Excerpts of journal entries and correspondence. Remember, as a friend or family member, you would be familiar with the daily concerns of your author's life. You would be acquainted with the writer's family, friends, teachers, and publisher.
- Information about the history and culture that affected your author's life and writing
- A critical review of the novel (or other literature) to understand the response to your author's writing

Reading Journal

You are required to keep a reading journal—a working space for notes, ideas, relevant page numbers, quotations, comments, and concerns. It is also a place to document your sources. Handwrite your reading journal and place it at the back of your portfolio.

Research Assignments

Relationship to Author

To define your relationship with your author, begin your reading and research. Once you have a sense of who your author is, choose your relationship and use this personal perspective to complete project assignments. If you don't wish to be a friend, you might consider the role of fellow artist, teacher, journalist, or family member.

Book Review

You will write a book review about the novel you read by your author. Your teacher will provide you with sample book reviews. Your class will analyze and discuss several book reviews to prepare you to write your own.

Glossary of Terms

Develop a glossary of words you encounter when researching your author's world: foreign words; slang; or vocabulary specific to geography, history, art, or food. Be sure each entry explains the relevance of the word to your author.

Circle of Friends

Assemble a gallery of photographs (or sketches) of your author's circle of friends and relatives. Include a photograph of yourself. Identify each person by name and profession (if possible).

Impressions of Author's Hometown or Geographical Region

With maps, photographs, and facts, portray a significant place where your author lived and worked. Using insights from your research, and the comments of the author's family and friends, demonstrate the importance of place (or the lack of it) to your writer. The place may include a region, urban or rural setting, the pleasures of home and garden, or passages from your writer's work that describe place.

Historical Events and Social Trends

Collect sample newspaper headlines, advertisements, and information about cultural events to provide a context for understanding your writer's response to the social and political issues of the day. Did the writer go to war, protest a political or social issue, or feel the effects of an economic downturn?

Organize photocopies of the artifacts you find (headlines, news articles, photographs) and combine them with commentary to clarify how history affected your author's life and work.

School libraries are generally a good source for reference books that reflect historical events and social trends.

Artistic Ideas

Research the effects of artistic and literary movements on your author (stream-of-consciousness, realism, cubism, surrealism, etc.)

and connect your author to other writers and artists of the period. To reflect the thinking of the times, use quotes or writing samples (of other authors) and display photocopies of sculpture or paintings.

Organize this section of your portfolio as a museum collection of work by writers and artists. Write comments about the collected works, linking ideas and inspiration between authors.

Letters to the Author

This section is an imaginary exchange of letters between you and your author. Remain in character as the author's friend (or family member, or whatever relationship you have chosen). Write at least two letters from the author's point of view and two in response. You may use photocopies of authentic letters written by your author if you are able to respond to their contents, or you may write the author's letters using the background information you have researched.

The Interview

The interview is a summation of what you have learned about your author. A fictitious journalist or scholar interviews you because of your friendship or other relationship with the author. You will develop interview questions about your author's writing and life and then respond to them, demonstrating your knowledge of the author. Type up your interview.

Portfolio

A portfolio is a showcase for your research project. All work is typed; examples of illustrations, photographs, and artwork are photocopied. Format and organize your packet with care. Please demonstrate pride in your work.

The following elements should be included in your portfolio:

Cover Page
The cover page is typed and formatted according to your teacher's specifications.

Table of Contents (typed)

Letter of Evaluation
In this letter, you will evaluate your portfolio according to the criteria that you have developed with your class. Your letter is the last assignment you will complete before turning in your portfolio, and your teacher will give you instructions on how to write it. Please insert this after the table of contents.

Annotated Bibliography

An annotated bibliography documents your sources and notes and demonstrates why they are relevant to your topic. Please type this.

Reading Journal

Insert your reading journal in the back of your portfolio. You do not need to type it. Think of it as your notes for the project.

Calendars

Insert the calendars you kept during the project. Don't try to type them.

Handwritten Annotations

On the day the portfolio is due, you will review your work in class and make handwritten comments on the pages (use Post-its if you wish). You may not want to ruin your beautifully typed packet by writing on it, but through this review, you will discover new insights. The informal comments you make in the margins will reflect the depth of your understanding.

7

Tracing the Protest Movement in America Through Song

A Scavenger Hunt

*One good song with a message can bring a point more deeply
to more people than a thousand rallies.*

—Phil Ochs

Teacher Instructions

One year, my students asked me so many questions about the music and protests of the sixties, I decided to develop a project on American protests. I am indebted to this group of students who piloted it and whose presentations were extravaganzas complete with live music, lights, and reenactments of protests in American history.

It turns out that the American protest song is a great vehicle for tracing protest movements throughout our history. These songs run the gamut from rock to folk music, although my abbreviated list sticks closely to my preference—songs generated in the folk tradition. It would be ideal to team this project with a history teacher, but since teaming is the exception and not the rule in American high schools, this often remains a literature project that is linked to history.

When students are researching, I usually ask them to map their research path graphically or in writing so that they can see how their choices led them to new information or brought them to a frustrating dead end. The process of getting students to be aware of the research path gave rise to the idea of the scavenger hunt, a context in which to frame student research. This project's first clue is derived from an analysis of the lyrics of a protest song, which leads students to a period in American history where they choose a focus: an event, a person, an organization, and so on.

Music Resources

As you repeat this project with your classes, you will begin to collect audiotapes, CDs, and folk music anthologies. With the advent of the Internet, there is easy access to lists of protest songs, history and criticism, and songbooks. Parents will contribute recordings, and college libraries are also a good resource. (School libraries usually cannot supply much of this material.)

Selecting Song Titles

I have provided a very basic song list for this project (see "Protest Song List" in Appendix E). It is no more than a sampling of a very long and complex list. Think about time periods or protest movements you wish to cover, from Colonialism to the present. Try to choose songs that have an obvious link to an era so students can connect their song to an event in history.

Of course, students will happily help you to compile your list by contributing rap and other contemporary genres. Much of it may be protest music, but my purpose is to use music as a link to events in American history.

Modifying the Project

This project can be modified for students who would find the entire project too challenging. With some background research on a protest song and its era, students can develop a musical presentation using a recording of the song, historical photographs, and quotes from people who participated in the protest.

Some students will actually perform the song on a guitar and many can write a simple song review.

Advanced students complete the entire project to give them an opportunity to organize research material from several subject areas and to develop a workable thesis.

Promoting Student-Centered Behaviors

Student-centered behaviors go hand in hand with academic success. Throughout the project, students teach punctuation, lead discussions, and help develop the criteria for evaluating writing, presentations, and graphics. When students revert to teacher dependence, remind them that they are working toward independent learning. Brainstorm solutions with them or suggest they collaborate with other students.

Set aside a bulletin board where students can post library hours, useful Web sites, and research questions another student may be able to answer.

Embedded Mini Lessons

Embedded mini lessons are "need-to-know" skills students confront as they move through the project, including punctuation, grammar, and endnotes.

Keeping a Calendar

Before you begin this project, block out a tentative calendar noting holidays, assemblies, and other interruptions. You will get a sense of where to embed mini lessons and student-led discussions as well as when students may have time to develop criteria or rubrics (see "Sample Teacher's Calendar" in Appendix E).

Once you have explained the project to your students, provide them with a blank calendar. As they move through the project, they will keep a daily record of what they have accomplished. Discuss tasks and due dates with your students so that everyone understands what is expected. The students will provide good feedback and the consensus of the class will be reasonable. On Mondays, before the class begins to work, agree upon what assignments will be completed during the week. On Fridays, develop a weekend plan to accomplish tasks outside of the classroom.

Keep a stack of blank calendars available for students to use (see "Blank Calendar" in Appendix A).

Additional Organization

Save yourself time by providing students with a bulletin board to share research information and a table with extra assignment sheets and reference books.

The Scavenger Hunt

Once you have decided on a list of protest songs, decide whether to give your students the option to work in pairs or individually. Team work has its obvious downside when a student doesn't contribute, but students completing this project without modification are usually very focused. Team work combines the strength of at least two individuals, provides an opportunity for instant feedback and improved revision and editing, and is generally the stronger approach. I give my students a choice. Make sure your students decide before they draw a song title. Then, follow these steps:

1. Cut up a list of song titles and place them in a hat.

2. Have students pull a song title from the hat. (Teams each use one song title.) Expect some good-natured bargaining as students trade songs.

3. Students begin the scavenger hunt by analyzing the title and lyrics of their song. They may also want to look up the songwriter or singer.

4. Pass out the worksheet, "Thinking About Your Protest Song," to help students analyze their song (see worksheet in Appendix E).

5. Students visit several libraries to research the protest movement and its history.

6. During the research process, use the "Questions for Class Discussion" (see worksheet in Appendix E). Set aside time for periodic student-led discussions. Students need to make distinctions between protest and breaking the law, and between violent and nonviolent protest, to clarify their own thinking in order to develop a thesis.

Song Review

If you are modifying the project, students write a review of their protest song, analyzing the lyrics and their significance. Provide them with a sample song review and remind them that they can use the information from the worksheet, "Thinking About Your Protest Song."

Essay

If students are going to complete the entire project, wait until they have completed the literature assignment and reading journal before having them choose between a song review and an essay (see assignment below). Advanced students often choose to write an essay.

Students may analyze the impact of the movement reflected by the song, the influence of an individual protest organizer, or the historical time period that incited the protest. They may also take a literary approach. As students research, they usually find a focus but will need help developing a thesis. A combination of peer and teacher instruction is usually necessary to develop well-crafted thesis statements.

As English teachers, we naturally focus on literary analysis. However, it is equally important to provide students with the tools for research papers in any subject area. Organizing research material and narrowing a topic is a tall order for most high school students. Student reports in history or science are too often just a summary of facts (if not plagiarism) rather than the development of a thesis. While we shouldn't expect an original thesis, we should demand that papers be written from a clearly defined perspective—this can be tricky and students need repeated practice.

Related Literature

Students read a novel, play, autobiography, biography, or a history of the time period of their protest song (they may also read a series of speeches). Obvious literary choices would include *The Scarlet Letter, The Crucible, The Adventures of Huckleberry Finn,* and *The Grapes of Wrath.* I want students to have the latitude to link the protest or historical period with the literature of the time because it is important they go through this discovery process. There is an abundance of autobiographies and biographies that work with this project, and history teachers are often very helpful if a student wishes to choose an historical novel or nonfiction selection.

Reading Journal

A reading journal authenticates the reading completed by a student and functions as a place to jot down ideas, make connections, ask questions, and note source information. You may also wish to provide students with a list of questions to ask of their reading and research. For example, this project lends itself to making connections between past protests and current events. You might also encourage students to interview a history teacher about a particular event. This would be the place for students to develop interview questions and write down the interviewee's answers. The reading journal is handwritten and placed at the back of the portfolio (see the following; see also "Reading Journal Instructions" in Appendix A).

Portfolio

A portfolio is a showcase for a student project, an organizational tool. The format is formal, and all work is typed. Artwork, photographs, and written samples are photocopied or illustrated and labeled. Prior to completing a portfolio, students develop the criteria and a rubric (if time permits) for evaluation purposes.

Cover Page (typed)
Teacher provides format.

Table of Contents (typed)

Letter of Evaluation (typed)
Students each write a letter of evaluation addressed to you, reflecting on the quality of their study habits and project assignments. Their ideas are supported by quotes from their written work and references to examples they have collected from other sources. The letter also covers use of time management and organization, the challenges of research, how and when the students asked for help and from whom, and what they would do differently if they were to complete another research project (see "Letter of Evaluation" questions in Appendix A).

Completed Worksheet: "Thinking About Your Protest Song"
(See worksheet in Appendix E.)

Song Review or Essay

Completed Student Worksheet: "Questions for Class Discussion"
(See worksheet in Appendix E.)

Annotated Bibliography (typed)
Students develop an annotated bibliography to document sources and illustrate their relevance. This should be typed.

Reading Journal
The reading journal is handwritten and placed at the back of the portfolio.

Handwritten Annotations
On the day the portfolio is due, students spend time in class reading their work. I ask them to make handwritten comments in the margins about sections they enjoyed or information they forgot to add. Some students are reluctant to do this because their portfolio is so neatly typed. However, some of their most interesting comments come from their informal observations after they have completed the project. This is also an opportunity for them to genuinely express what sections of the project they enjoyed.

Calendar

Students insert the calendar they kept during the project. This should be handwritten, not typed.

Timeline Graphic

Using a poster board, students develop a graphic representation of their protest song using slogans, symbols, and words to identify the song and its era. The song title and date it was written are placed in the right-hand bottom corner of the poster board. The class agrees on specific graphic design requirements before beginning their timeline poster. For example, they may want the lettering used for the song title and date to be uniform. When the graphics are complete, they are put up on the classroom wall in chronological order to create a timeline.

Ideas for Creating the Timeline Graphic

Since students usually approach a poster board project without much thought to design, ask them to make a sketch before beginning their poster board. Here are some suggestions you might offer to help them:

- Suggest that they try to fill the entire poster board—don't let images drown in large white spaces.
- Tell them not to type a list of encyclopedic facts because they cannot be seen and read easily from a distance.
- Remind students to present information thematically.
- Encourage the use of symbols, slogans, song titles, and lyrics.
- Make sure the song title and date are written in the lower right-hand corner of the poster board.

Presentation

The first time my class and I tried this unit, I asked for 3- to 5-minute presentations. That is not what I got. Instead, we moved to the choir room where there was a good sound system, a piano, and lighting, and the students put on quite an elaborate show. However, presentations certainly don't need to turn into full-blown dramas. You can insist that students stick to the 5-minute rule by asking them to integrate the protest song, their graphic, and some historical perspective into a monologue, dialogue, or speech. A student who wishes to sing his or her song live is still afforded the opportunity, and students can use costumes if they wish. As a last resort, students can do a straight presentation. Whatever you decide, it is a good idea to videotape the presentations when possible. Students will enjoy watching and critiquing them after the fact.

Student Instructions

The purpose of this research project is to explore how protest songs reflect important events in American history.

The Scavenger Hunt

1. Decide whether you would like to work alone or with a partner.

2. Pull a song title from the hat. If you are working with a partner, pull only one title.

3. To begin this research project, analyze the song using the questions from the worksheet, "Thinking About Your Protest Song." This information should lead you to related history; popular culture; literature; advertising; economics; and in some cases, inventions.

4. Visit several libraries to research the connection between your protest song and history.

5. Use the worksheet, "Questions for Class Discussion," so that you may prepare for and contribute to several student-led class discussions.

Song Review

If you are completing this project up to this section, you will write a review of your protest song analyzing the lyrics and their historical significance. You many also use the questions you answered on the worksheet, "Thinking About Your Protest Song." Your teacher will provide you with a sample song review.

Essay

If you are going to complete the entire project, wait until you have read the literature assignment and finished a reading journal before choosing between a song review and an essay (see assignment below).

You may approach the essay from one of several perspectives. Choose from the following: analyze the impact of a protest movement;

explore the influence of an individual protest organizer; or examine the historical factors that contributed to the protest. You may also take a literary approach and analyze a theme or character in the novel you read. As you research, jot down ideas you might use as the focus of your paper for the development of a thesis.

Related Literature

You may choose to read a novel, play, autobiography, biography, or a history of the time period related to your protest song. Your task is to link the protest song or historical period with a specific piece of literature. Your English and history teachers can provide you with suggestions, but try making the connection yourself before asking them. Write down several reading choices and then decide which suits you. If you are concerned that your parents might object to your choice, discuss it with them.

Reading Journal

You will keep a reading journal as a working space for notes, ideas, page numbers, quotations, comments, and concerns as well as citation information. It also authenticates the reading you have completed. Do not worry about typing your reading journal; it may be handwritten and placed at the back of your portfolio.

Portfolio

A portfolio is a showcase for your research project. All work is to be typed (with the exception of the reading journal and the calendar); examples should be photocopied, photographed, or drawn. Format and organize your portfolio with care. Please demonstrate pride in your work.

Your portfolio should include the following elements:

Cover Page (typed)
The cover page is typed and formatted according to your teacher's specifications.

Table of Contents (typed)

Letter of Evaluation (typed)
In this letter, you will evaluate your portfolio according to the criteria that your class has developed with the help of your teacher. Your letter is the last assignment you will complete before turning in your portfolio. Please insert this after the cover page.

Completed Worksheet: "Thinking About Your Protest Song"

Song Review or Essay

Completed Worksheet: "Questions for Class Discussion"

Annotated Bibliography (typed)

An annotated bibliography documents your sources and demonstrates why they are relevant to your topic. Please type this.

Handwritten Annotations

On the day the project is due, you will have time to review your work and make handwritten comments on the pages of your project. You may be reluctant to ruin your beautifully typed portfolio by writing on it, but through such a review, you will discover new insights about your research. Your informal, spontaneous comments will often demonstrate your new understanding of the subject.

Reading Journal

Insert your reading journal in the back of your portfolio. You do not need to type it. Think of it as your notes for the project.

Calendar

Once you understand the requirements for this project, use a calendar to note assignment due dates. You will discuss assignments and due dates weekly with your teacher. You will also decide what homework you need to complete for the weekend. Place this calendar behind your reading journal in your portfolio. Don't try to type it.

Timeline Graphic

1. Each member of your class (or you and a partner) designs a poster board that represents your protest song by using slogans, symbols, and words to identity the song and its era.

2. As a class, you may decide upon certain design elements. For example, you may want the title of your song and the date to be a uniform size or color.

3. The title of your song and the date it was written are placed in the bottom right-hand corner of the poster board. Make sure the lettering is large enough to be seen by the entire classroom.

4. When the graphics are complete, they are put up on the classroom wall in chronological order to create a timeline.

Presentation

Your presentation must integrate the following:

- An excerpt of the words of your protest song;
- An understanding of the protest issue, and related history and literature.

In addition, you may want to do any of the following:

- Add photographs, use your poster board graphic, or dress in costume, or use observations made by someone who lived through the protest or the time period.
- You may provide an audio sample of your protest song. (In the interest of time, you should not play the entire song, although you might use it as background music for your presentation.)
- You may give a live performance of your song.

Think carefully about a method of presentation that allows you a good way to present your material. If you are inclined to be theatrical, you may want to give a monologue, develop a dialogue, use students in the audience as protesters, or give a fiery protest speech. Of course, you also have the choice of giving a straightforward presentation.

Using the criteria the class has developed for evaluating the presentations, you will receive feedback from classmates as well as from your teacher.

8

Case Studies

Younger Students

All students need to practice "student-centered" behaviors in a less complex context than an entire project where multiple English skills and time management issues are required of them. Reading a piece of literature or working on writing helps students maintain a single academic focus while incorporating student-centered behaviors. The academic focus can be challenging, as it is here where sophomores are learning to write a reflective essay.

Focusing Writing Strategies for a Reflective Essay

Background

First-period sophomore English is made up of a preponderance of low-achieving students who have, with some reluctance, made an effort to participate in "student-centered" behaviors. For these students, it is especially important to practice behaviors that are both active and appropriate for the classroom—and to repeat this practice often so that they know what is expected of them.

This particular class has been studying writing and making the transition from narrative to reflective essay. They have participated in student-led discussions, used student-developed criteria to evaluate their discussions, and worked hard to intentionally support each other through peer tutoring.

This writing project is meant to allow students the time to internalize the writing strategies needed to write a reflective essay. To do this, they analyze essays written by students and professionals, use the technical writing terms to talk about the essays, and ultimately analyze a reflective essay in a student-led discussion group before beginning to write their own reflective essay.

Students Need Choices

When introducing abstract concepts, this class needs choices to feel comfortable. If students feel confused or pressured, they will give up. They generally enjoy graphics and so I offer them this option: "We will map out the writing strategies in this essay together. You do it on your piece of paper, while I do it on the overhead."

For students who quickly grasp the concepts or who are creative and want to develop their own graphic, I give them the opportunity to work independently.

Students who are unable to decide how they wish to work will typically follow along with the graphic developed on the overhead.

Sample Questions

Here are some questions to ask as you map out the writing strategies in the essay:

"I think this is an example of personal reflection. What do you think?"

"Would you like to read that sentence?"

"Could the writer improve on it? In what way?"

"What icon would you like to use to represent personal reflection?"

"Would you like to come up to the overhead and draw it on the overhead next to the personal reflection?"

Enlist the Vocal Students as Teachers

Larry, my vocal student, observes that the essay is boring.

"Who cares about the girl's bicycle ride?"

"Perhaps the writer is being careful to use the writing strategies she has learned," I suggest.

"Yeah, well, there are better subjects."

"Don't be so critical, you haven't written your essay yet," says Lacy, a student who is proud of her writing skills.

"Perhaps you would like to volunteer to help us understand one of the writing strategies," I suggest to Larry. He sighs, looks around the classroom, and then asks, "You mean be a teacher?"

"Yes. As long as the class can follow you."

"Yeah, I'll make it crazy."

"Would you like to team teach with another student?"

"I will work with him," volunteers Lacy. Larry smiles.

Expect Students to Participate

"I need one more teacher," I say, looking around the classroom. The students look at each other. The classroom grows quiet. I sit down in a chair to wait them out. Suddenly, the bell rings and students gather up their backpacks and look nervously at the clock. "OK, OK, I'll do it," agrees Miranda.

"Do you want to work with another student?"

"No, I'm good."

Review What Occurred the Day Before

(Ask a student to write important information on the board.)

"Let's review our objective and write down the names of the students who will teach the writing strategies for the reflective essay. Roberto, will you write the student teachers' names on the board?"

Typically, there will be some confusion at the beginning of a project—not so much because students don't understand what is expected of them, but because they can't believe what is expected of them.

"You're crazy. You want us to act like college students."

"This is too much work. I can't do this."

"I can't decide what poet to study."

"I can't find a novel."

Once students understand the project and are deeply involved in a specific aspect of it, they will be driven crazy by a teacher who repeats the project objective and daily instructions at each class session. A class will begin to demonstrate self-starting behavior after about three days of repeating one project activity (e.g., reading and reading journal, research, graphics, etc.).

"We know what we have to do!" they say, coming through the door.

"Good. Who would like to state the objective for this reading assignment?"

Hands go up.

"OK, Yesenia, what is the objective for this assignment?"

"We read to our partner and answer questions in our reading journal," she answers.

"Why are we doing this?"

"We're trying to understand the story for the class discussion."

"Good. Please write that on the board." (The objective does not need to sound like a teacher wrote it.)

(The next day)

"What are we going to do today?" a student asks.

Juan pipes up with an answer. "We are going to use our reading journals to talk about the story."

"Does everyone understand what Juan just said?" I ask the class. "Are there any questions?"

"Can we go to work now?" a student asks.

On the other hand, confusion can occur because of a lack of clarification on the teacher's part. For example, I am helping student teachers prepare their lessons, while the remainder of the class works in groups developing the criteria for student-led discussion. In this interaction, two different groups are working on two different issues and a student comes up with something I hadn't thought of. This confusion becomes an interruption and students lean on me for answers and lose their independence. This situation is my fault and I say so.

(I am helping the student teachers prepare to teach in a corner of the classroom.)

"Do I have to write on the overhead?" asks Larry.

"Not necessarily. How would you like to convey the information?"

"I would like to . . ." Larry begins.

(A student across the room working to develop criteria interrupts.)

"Can't we use the criteria from our last student-led discussion?"

"Of course," I say, "but you need to refine them."

"What does that mean?"

"I know what she means," says another student in the group. "You got to use less words or maybe add something to them."

"Stop," I say at this point. "We've interrupted the discussions by talking across the classroom. Class, can you give us a moment to sort this out?" (The class quiets down.)

"Thanks. I should have made it clear that you can use any resources in the classroom you can find, whether they were developed by teachers or students. Use them as samples to build on criteria you have already developed."

"Where are the criteria that we made for our last discussion?" a student asks.

"I'd like to ask you why you are relying on me for copies of the criteria for the last discussion, when you know where they are kept."

"You are supposed to solve the problems," someone says good-naturedly. (The class laughs.)

"I ain't your mama," I say and smile. "How are we going to get back on track?"

"Let the facilitators worry about group problems," suggests someone.

"Class?"

"Yeah, OK."

Transitions from one activity to the next within the framework of a project typically flow (analysis of reflective essays as a class—student teachers teach writing strategies—development of criteria for a small-group student-led discussion—student-led discussions—evaluation of student-led discussions—students write reflective essay). When the activities do not flow, it is usually because students need more time to complete a variety of activities. A catch-up day is OK, as long as everyone has something to do.

Working With Students on Time Management

"Tomorrow our student teachers will review the writing strategies used in a reflective essay. Are we ready?"

"I need another example of new awareness," says one student.

"The video camera is being used tomorrow—we can't have it until Wednesday," adds another.

"We are still refining the discussion criteria," another student pipes in.

"It sounds to me like you need more time. Is that what I am hearing?"

"Yeah, we need another day," the class agrees.

"If we wait until Wednesday to hear from our teachers, can we agree that your work will be completed by the end of tomorrow's class session? Do you all have a focus for tomorrow? I will put our list of suggested topics for reflective essays on the board just in case you need to begin the next task."

Videotaping student-led discussions formalizes both the discussions and the classroom behavior. The video camera becomes an excellent mirror for students who cannot seem to take responsibility for their behavior or who honestly don't realize how they look. Derek, for example, wears his hat backwards, his pants "sag," and he carries an open Coke can. He is late for class, slams the classroom door as he enters, and walks directly in front of the camera, interrupting a student-led discussion.

The class groans as Derek walks in.

"Oh man, I'm sorry," Derek says. "Oh, that's awful."

Another student suggests, "Derek should see what he looks like."

"Derek, what do you think?" I ask him.

Derek shrugs. The cameraperson plays the video.

"I look awful," Derek whispers and seems genuinely dismayed.

Whole-Class Literature Discussion for High School Juniors

The Adventures of Huckleberry Finn

This is a large junior class with students of mixed abilities. They have been in my class for about three months and like to participate in class discussions and projects. They have held small-group, student-led discussion, but this is their first attempt at holding a literature discussion with the entire class, independent of me. Two students have volunteered to teach Chapters 7 and 8 of *The Adventures of Huckleberry Finn* and a student has volunteered to evaluate the discussion.

To prepare for the discussion, the students read chapters and work in small groups to develop literal and interpretative questions, as well as questions that are related to the students' lives. The questions are written on three different colors of Post-its and stuck to the white board.

Sample Questions

Literal question: Whose blood did Huck use in the cabin to make his father think he was dead?

Interpretative question: Why do you think Jim is superstitious?

Question related to students' life: What kinds of things would you do to survive on Jackson Island?

A student organizes the questions and gives them to the two students who will act as teachers. The teachers edit them and pass out a list of questions for class review.

During the discussion, students must back up their opinions with quotes from the chapters, and to prepare, they again work in small groups to find appropriate quotes and note page numbers. In the meantime, the student teachers go through a similar process and work on strategies for engaging the class in the discussion. One teacher will ask the questions for the first half of the hour and the other will monitor the class, repeating questions and answers and making sure a variety of students participate. Halfway through the discussion, the teachers exchange roles.

Students have developed and agreed upon criteria for the class discussion. Their focus will be to keep the discussion away from me through their participation and ability to solve their own problems. The class understands that to be successful, everyone must know the literature.

Student-Led Class Discussion

To begin the discussion, the first teacher reviews Chapter 6 and Pap's drunken rampage.

First teacher: "Please turn to page 29. I'll start the discussion by reading the bottom paragraph. 'Pap was ago-ing on so, he never noticed where his old limber legs was taking him to, so he went head over heels over the tub of salt pork.' Huck seems pretty smart, but is he in control when his father is drunk?"

A student: "No. In Chapter 6, on page 31, third complete paragraph, Huck says of his father, 'He chased me round and round the place, with a clasp-knife, calling me the Angel of Death and saying he would kill me.'"

Another student:	"Yeah, but he gains control again when Pap is sobered up."
First teacher:	"Can you find a paragraph in Chapter 7 that shows this?"
Student:	"On page 34, Huck escapes by using his head. In the first complete paragraph, last sentence, Huck says, 'Before [Pap] was tother side of the river I was out of the hole; him and his raft was just a speck on the water away off yonder.'"
Another student:	"Huck also takes food and supplies. In the second complete paragraph on 34, he lists what he took."
First teacher:	"Read a little of that paragraph."
Student:	"'I took the sack of corn meal. . . . I took the wadding; I took the bucket and gourd.'"
First teacher:	"So, Huck is good at surviving. Would you have killed a wild pig to use its blood?"
A student:	"We're not used to doing that sort of thing."
Another student:	"I would have."
First teacher:	"Is the scene believable—do you really think Pap and later the town would really think Huck was dead by looking at the blood?"
Student:	"Would you repeat the question?"
Second teacher:	"Wouldn't Pap or the town ask some questions before pronouncing Huck dead?"
First teacher:	"The other question is whether Mark Twain cared if the scene was believable."
Student:	"I think we should go back and discuss the first question."
First teacher:	"OK."
Evaluator:	"You guys knew the material well and used quotes most of the time. You kept the discussion away from Ms. Hickman, which was your goal. The teachers did a good job of calling on a variety of students and the class moved the discussion forward when it started to go in circles. I liked that students asked to have some of the questions repeated.

	To improve your discussion, I'd say that you need to shorten the parts of the discussion that have to do with your personal experience. The focus should mainly be about the book. Also, when you are reading passages from the book, just read the sentences that support your idea. You guys lose your focus if you read too much."
Another student:	"I know this is hard to do, but I think that the teachers should repeat the comments that the students make. That would make it easier for us to acknowledge what was said or add to it."
Evaluator:	"Yes. That is the job of the teacher who is not teaching. Do you have any questions or comments?"
Student:	"How would you evaluate the discussion?"
Evaluator:	"I would say it was 'proficient.' You met your goal of being independent of the teacher, although the discussion was a little stiff—like you were scared."
Student:	"Naw, we weren't scared. It is hard to refer to the quotes and keep the discussion going."
Evaluator:	"What do you think, Ms. Hickman?"
Ms. Hickman:	"I was pleased with the discussion and very proud of you. In fact, I probably would not be as hard on you as the evaluator, but he does have a point. There were times when reading passages from the book seemed to replace the discussion. However, there is no question in my mind that you guys have read carefully and put a lot of effort into this discussion. We'll watch the videotape tomorrow."

Resources

Appendix A

Project Design

Project Format

Title of Project

Appropriate Quote

Portfolio Assignments

Description of Project:

Cover Page

Table of Contents

Section 1 Assignments

Thesis

Analysis

Section 2 Assignments

More analysis

Section 3 Assignments

Section 4 Making Other Connections

Literature connected to other subject areas—art, music history, science, math

Section 5

Essay

Annotated Bibliography

Reading or Dialectical Journal

Handwritten Annotations

Presentation

Blank Calendar

Monday	Tuesday	Wednesday	Thursday	Friday
■ Presentations				

Reading Journal Instructions

A reading journal helps you to think about the book that you are reading by asking you to jot down your thoughts about what you are reading and how it is written. The questions below are sample questions to get you started thinking about your novel. Please pay attention to how the author writes and use quotes from the text to support your ideas.

1. As you read, decide which characters make you think about yourself, your friends, and family. Do the characters remind you of characters in the movies or on television?

2. Do you love to hate the villain(s) in the novel? Do you feel sorry for the victims, and are you interested in the outcasts who don't seem to find their place in society?

3. Of the places described in the novel, which place would you choose to live? How does the author describe this place?

4. If you were a character in this novel, who would you be and why?

5. Describe this character's philosophy of life. Select a dialogue or description that portrays this character's beliefs about a specific conflict or general view of life.

6. How does this character treat other characters in the novel? Describe a specific relationship that you feel is important to the story.

7. How does this character attempt to resolve a conflict? How would you resolve a similar conflict?

8. Is there a character that changes dramatically during the course of the novel? Is this change believable?

9. Does the novel deal with issues that transcend individual characters and express a universal human experience?

10. If you were to give this novel to a friend to read, what would you say about it?

Dialectical Journal

Quote From Literature	Your Comment

Graduation Speech Worksheet

This is your chance to think about your educational experience through the twelfth grade and grapple with the issues and challenges of the adult world. The following ideas are intended to get you thinking about topics for your graduation speech. Please do not fill your speech with clichés about the past and future. Reflect upon your school experiences and then deal with one substantive issue that your generation will confront. Issues might include environmental, educational, or health issues, as well as poverty and ongoing conflicts around the world. Be sure to do your research and back up your ideas with facts.

Introduction

You might choose to do the following:

- Relate a personal anecdote
- Quote someone
- Issue a challenge
- Make a startling statement

Body

Connect your introduction to your research topic. State the problem or challenge and the facts. Build toward a major point. Use some reflection, but don't overdo it. Do not address every aspect of an issue. You are limited to 5 minutes.

Conclusion

Remind your audience of the importance of your topic. Invite them to participate in resolving the issue. Return to your role as a graduate and how you will confront the future.

Sample Student Scheduling Graphic

Scheduling
(Overhead transparency)

Students	Dates	Teachers
Sam James Maria Chavez Ann Kline	Dec. 3 & 4	Bill & Monica
Debbie Littleton Brandon Smith Janice Sanders	Dec. 5 & 6	Connie & Heather
Ted Brown Luis Mendoza Don Mead	Dec. 9 & 10	Jatinder & Brian
Hector Sanchez Alejandro Medina Susan Brighton	Dec. 11 & 12	Mike & Mysti
Lauren Hall James Merritt Tonya Tipton	Dec. 13 &16	Jamie & Kim
Dana Dewitt Greg Sharwood	Dec. 17 & 18	Ed & Dasha

Letter of Evaluation

(Date)

Dear (Teacher's Name):

During this project (or semester),

1. I enjoyed . . .
   (quote from student's work and commentary)

2. I disliked . . .
   (quote from student's work and commentary)

3. I had difficulty with . . .
   (quote from student's work and commentary)

4. My time management and organizational skills were . . .

5. I was a peer tutor, led a discussion, helped develop a rubric, etc. These activities . . .

6. If I were to do this project over again, I would . . .

7. I would improve the project by . . .

   For example . . .

8. Other. (You may request feedback about a specific idea, or students might want to add a personal note.)

Sincerely,

(Student's Name)

Progress Memo

To:

From:

Date:

Project:

Subject:

_____

Progress:

Questions:

Problems:

Appendix B

Adopt a Poet

Adopt-A-Poet Tentative Calendar

Sample Teacher's Calendar

Monday	Tuesday	Wednesday	Thursday	Friday	Saturday
• Pass out research checklist • Review requirements and outcomes • Hand out lists of American and/or British poets • Peruse literature textbooks for poets	Visit school library (Before going to the library, review tasks)	Visit school library	• Return to classroom • Review research progress • Clarify assignment • Allow students to read and/or organize materials that they have found • Some students will need to peruse literature textbooks	• Discuss and develop for more research • Allow majority of students to read their research materials in classroom • Assign mini lessons: annotated bibliography, analyze poem, presentation	**Weekend plan** • Visit public and/or university libraries
• Check student progress on research • Student-led mini lesson on annotated bibliography • Read	• Total immersion in research • Read poems by poet • Read biographical material • Look for historical and artistic influences	• Total immersion in research • Read poems by poet • Read biographical material • Look for historical and artistic influences	• Brainstorm how to come up with a unifying theme • Check student progress	• Discuss student progress • Students share ideas for a unifying theme • Develop weekend plan	**Weekend plan** • Visit public and/or university libraries • Refine unifying theme • Choose poem to analyze

Monday	Tuesday	Wednesday	Thursday	Friday	Saturday
• Student-led mini lesson on analyzing a poem • Teacher expansion of this lesson	• Read a poem and brainstorm on thesis • Pass out a literary essay as a model • Read and discuss	• Brainstorm thesis for poem • Share several thesis statements on overhead and discuss	• Help individual students to develop thesis statements • Draft supporting paragraphs	• Work on essay • Help individual students • Develop weekend plan	**Weekend plan** • Work on essay • Work on annotated bibliography
• Students develop criteria for evaluating essays • Peer evaluations • Revise essays	• Revise essays • Help students individually	• Pass out checklists on graphics and presentations • Review	• Essay due • Work on dummy graphic layout	• Develop weekend plan • Work on dummy graphic layout	**Weekend plan** • Complete graphic
• Student-led lesson on the development of a presentation • Teacher expansion of this lesson • Return graded essay	• Develop outline of presentation synthesizing all research information and requirements of project • Check outlines	• Memorize poem and work on presentation rehearsal • Practice in groups	• Memorize poem and work on presentation rehearsal • Practice in groups • Select volunteers for practice presentations • List criteria for evaluating presentations	• Listen to two volunteer presentations • Break into groups and discuss presentations • Develop rubric for evaluation	**Weekend plan** • Practice presentations
Presentations	Presentations	Presentations	Presentations	Presentations	

Teacher's Project Checklist

☐ Review the project with students.

☐ Share student work from past years if you have it.

☐ Block out a tentative project calendar for yourself and then again with your students.

☐ Share books and other teacher resources you may have in the classroom that feature poets.

☐ Ask the school librarian to display poetry collections.

☐ Spend several days in the school library researching.

☐ When students return to the classroom, ask them to share their research.

☐ On Mondays, discuss project expectations for the week.

☐ Monitor student work frequently.

☐ Embed student-led discussions, peer tutoring, and the development of criteria and rubrics into the project timeline.

☐ Embed skill-based lessons into the research process; review student progress and adjust due dates accordingly.

☐ Evaluate sections of the project as students complete assignments.

Student Presentation Checklist

☐ My presentation is based on the following idea:

☐ My idea was developed (a) in my essay, (b) in my graphic, (c) both.

☐ I introduce my presentation by
  - Reciting the poem,
  - Providing background information,
  - Quoting my poet,
  - Introducing an interesting idea,
  - Other (please explain).

☐ I successfully integrate the biographical information into my presentation, by . . .
  (Note: Make sure you don't give a biographical report.)

☐ I include this event/person/artwork because . . .

☐ During my presentation, I use my poster board
  - As a map to guide me through my presentation,
  - To make a point,
  - Other (please explain).

☐ I practiced my presentation in front of the following people:

☐ I can recite the poem by heart.

☐ I will use the following equipment during my presentation: (overhead, PowerPoint, audio or videotape, etc.)

Poster Board Checklist

☐ I have completed all the necessary research for my graphic.

☐ My poet wrote poems about . . .

☐ I will use the poem or an idea of interest to the poet as the centerpiece of my graphic.

☐ I will use my concrete poem to represent the poem on the poster board.

☐ I have integrated biographical information into the design by . . .

☐ I will use the following quote to represent the poet's ideas about writing:

☐ I will design my poster board using the following idea from my essay:

☐ My poet's name appears boldly in the lower right-hand corner of the poster board.

☐ I have sketched out a preliminary design for my poster board and have gotten feedback from classmates and the teacher.

☐ An annotated bibliography is attached to the back of my poster board.

☐ I can think of ways to use my poster board as a prop when I give my presentation. I might use it this way:

☐ My work on this poster board project reflects my very best effort. Comment:

Sample of Concrete Poetry

Appendix C

Project Monster

Sample Teacher's Calendar

Project Monster Tentative Calendar

Monday	Tuesday	Wednesday	Thursday	Friday	Saturday
Review student instructions • Brainstorm a list of monsters in literature • Show examples of portfolios (if you have them)	**Visit school library** • Meet in library • Help students find books for their projects		• Return to classroom • Students share their books and ideas for projects • Students fill out book contract • Review purpose of reading journal • Students begin to read and work in reading journal	• Students continue to read and work in reading journal • Develop weekend plan	**Weekend plan** • Continue to read monster literature • Work in reading journal • Visit public or college library
• Check reading progress • Clarify project and answer questions • All students need to have filled out a book contract • Students read and work in reading journal	• Students read and work in reading journal • Encourage students to use their reading journal to work on ideas for project	• Students read and work in reading journal	• Review requirements for portfolio (*do this often; it takes awhile for students to understand what is required of them*)	• Students read and work in reading journal • Develop weekend plan	**Weekend plan** • Continue to read and work in reading journal
• Pass out sample book reviews • Appoint a student to lead discussion on Tuesday • Students read book review silently to prepare for discussion	• Student-led discussion on how to write a book review (*see unit on student-led discussion*) • Students begin book review • Due date Friday	• Students work on book review or components of projects	• Review requirements for portfolio • Peer edit book reviews	• Students turn in book reviews • Check student progress • Develop weekend plan	**Weekend plan** • Continue to visit libraries • Work on components of project

114

Monday	Tuesday	Wednesday	Thursday	Friday	Saturday
• Students work on components of their project					
• Return book reviews and discuss • Pass out annotated bibliography review • Students work on components of their project	• Students bring portfolio to class • Students spend the hour writing a letter of evaluation • Students copy portions of their packet they may need for their presentations	• Students annotate portfolio • Students share portfolios with each other • Turn in portfolios	• Students begin to develop their presentation	• Brainstorm ideas for presentations • "Meeting of the Minds" monologues • Dialogue • Hot seat • Interview • Develop weekend plan • Students work on presentation • Student write up presentation plan and a needs list (overhead, tape recorder, etc.)	**Weekend plan** • Practice presentation
• Check progress on presentations	• Students practice presentations with classmates	• Begin presentations • Students evaluate presentations according to the criteria they have developed	**Presentations** (continue through the next week)		

Teacher's Project Checklist

☐ Block out a tentative project calendar.

☐ Collect books and other resources to help students choose a monster or the appropriate literature.

☐ Speak to the school librarian and other teachers who might be a resource to students during this project.

☐ Provide an overview of the project to the class.

☐ Brainstorm a list of monsters and classic literature with the class (this will save time).

☐ Share projects from past classes if you have them.

☐ Visit the school library several times.

☐ Return to the classroom and provide time for students to share project ideas and resources.

☐ Organize small-group discussions to facilitate student commitment to an author.

☐ Ask students to fill out a book contract.

☐ Each Monday, make a plan with your students about work expectations.

☐ Ask students to keep a record of their daily accomplishments on a calendar that you provide.

☐ Develop a weekend plan with your students each Friday.

☐ Use peer tutoring to help struggling students.

☐ Monitor student work frequently by signing off on specific assignments.

☐ Embed student-centered behaviors.

☐ Use skill-based assignments during the project (grammar, punctuation, documentation, annotated bibliography, book review format, etc.).

☐ Grade assignments as they are completed.

☐ Pick up the pace between portfolio due date and the development of the presentation. (Students need the momentum to complete their presentations.)

☐ Provide students with opportunities to improve assignments to work toward mastery.

☐ Set up a student resource bulletin board and table in the classroom.

Student Checklist

☐ I understand the project requirements.

☐ I have chosen a monster to research and have filled out the book contract.

☐ I have found sufficient research material to complete this project.

☐ I keep a calendar of assignments and due dates.

☐ I have completed an assignment from Section 1 of the project, "Introduce Your Monster."

☐ I have completed an assignment from Section 2 of my project, "Analysis."

☐ I have completed an assignment from Section 3 of my project, "More Analysis."

☐ I have completed an assignment from Section 4 of my project, "Making Other Connections."

☐ I have completed the essay.

☐ I have completed an annotated bibliography.

☐ I have completed my letter of evaluation.

☐ My portfolio is a formal research document that is prepared and formatted correctly.

☐ I have given my presentation and read the peer evaluations.

☐ I have listened to my classmates' presentations and have evaluated them using criteria developed by the class.

☐ I have facilitated a student-led discussion or taught a mini lesson.

Teacher Resource List of Books and Movies

Science as Monster

Dr. Jekyll and Mr. Hyde (1886) (Robert Louis Stevenson) Book/
  Many Movies
Frankenstein (1931) (Mary Shelley) Book/Movie
The Invisible Man (1933) (H.G. Wells) Book/Movie
The Island of Dr. Moreau (1896) (H.G. Wells) Book/Movies: *Island of
  Lost Souls* (1933), *The Island of Dr. Moreau* (1977; 1996)
Bride of Frankenstein (1935) Movie
Dr. Cyclops (1940) Movie
Donovan's Brain (1953) Movie
20,000 Leagues Under the Sea (1954) (Jules Verne) Book/Movie
Them! (1954) Movie
Godzilla, King of the Monsters (1954) Movie
The Incredible Shrinking Man (1957) Movie
Mysterious Island (1961) (Jules Verne) Book/Movie
The Fly (1958; 1986) Movies
The Stepford Wives (1975) (Ira Levin) Book/Movie (2004)
The Andromeda Strain (1981) (Michael Crichton) Book/Movie
Videodrome (1983) Movie
Jurassic Park (1993) (Michael Crichton) Book/Movie

Android/Robot/Computer as Monster

2001: A Space Odyssey (1968) (Arthur C. Clarke) Book/Movie
Colossus, the Forbin Project (1970) Movie
Westworld (1973) Movie
Demon Seed (1977) (Dean Koontz) Book/Movie
Tron (1982) Movie

Aliens as Monster

The Thing (1951; 1982) Movies
War of the Worlds (1898) (H.G. Wells)
  Book/Movies(1953; 2005)
Invaders From Mars (1953) Movie
Invasion of the Body Snatchers (1956; 1978) Movies
Earth vs. the Flying Saucers (1956) Movie
The Blob (1958) Movie
The Midwich Cuckoos (1957) (John Wyndham) Book/Movie: *Village
  of the Damned* (1960)
Day of the Triffids (1963) (John Wyndham) Book/Movie

Independence Day (1996) Movie
Signs (2002) Movie

Nature as Monster

King Kong (1933; 2005) Movies
Creature From the Black Lagoon (1954) Movie
The Naked Jungle (1954) Movie
The Birds (1963) (Daphne du Maurier) Book/Movie
Phase IV (1974) Movie
Jaws (1975) (Peter Benchley) Book/Movie

Supernatural as Monster

The Mummy (1932; 1998) Movies
The Wolf Man (1941) Movie
The Cat People (1942; 1982) Movies
Beast With Five Fingers (1947) Movie
Curse of the Demon (1952) Movie
Masque of the Red Death (1842) (Edgar Allan Poe) Short Story/
    Movie (1964)
Carrie (1976) (Stephen King) Book/Movie
An American Werewolf in London (1981) Movie
Silver Bullet (1985) (Stephen King) Book/Movie

Satan as Monster

Rosemary's Baby (1968) (Ira Levin) Book/Movie
The Omen (1976) Movie

Vampire as Monster

Nosferatu (1922) Book (Based on *Dracula*)/Movie (1979)
Dracula (1931) (Bram Stoker) Book/Movies (1979; 1992)
Lost Boys (1987) Movie
Near Dark (1987) Movie
Buffy the Vampire Slayer (1992) Movie

Witches as Monster

Macbeth (William Shakespeare) Play/Many Movies
The Wizard of Oz (1939) (L. Frank Baum) Book/Movie
Return to Oz (1985) Movie (Loosely based on book, *The Land of Oz*)
Conjure Wife (1962) (Fritz Leiber)/Movie: *Burn, Witch, Burn* (1962)
The Witches (1989) (Roald Dahl) Book/Movie
The Blair Witch Project (1999) Movie

Ghosts as Monster

The Turn of the Screw (1898) (Henry James) Book/Movie: *The Innocents* (1961)

The Haunting of Hill House (1963) (Shirley Jackson) Book/Movie: *The Haunting* (1999)

The Legend of Hell House (1973) (Richard Matheson) Book/Movie

The Amityville Horror (1979) Movie

The Shining (1980) (Stephen King) Book/Movie

Poltergeist (1982) Movie

The Sixth Sense (1999) Movie

The Others (2001) Movie

The Ring (2002) Movie

The Ring 2 (2005) Movie

The Grudge (2004) Movie

The Grudge 2 (2006) Movie

System as Monster

Les Misérables (Victor Hugo) Book/Many Movies

Metropolis (1927) Movie

1984 (1954) (George Orwell) Book/Movie (1984)

Animal Farm (1955) (George Orwell) Book/Movie

The Manchurian Candidate (1962) (Richard Condon) Book/Movies (1962; 2004)

Dr. Strangelove (1964) Movie

Fahrenheit 451 (1966) (Ray Bradbury) Book/Movie

Soylent Green (1973) Movie

Society as Monster

The Scarlet Letter (1850) (Nathaniel Hawthorne) Book/Movie (1995)

Freaks (1932) Movie

The Crucible (1953) (Arthur Miller) Play/Movie (1996)

"The Lottery" (Shirley Jackson) Short Story

Rebel Without a Cause (1955) Movie

Lord of the Flies (1963) (William Golding) Book/Movie (1990)

Psyche as Monster

M (1930) Movie

The Picture of Dorian Gray (1891) (Oscar Wilde) Book/Movie (1945)

Night of the Hunter (1955) Movie

The Bad Seed (1956) Play/Movie

Psycho (1960) (Robert Bloch) Book/Movie

Cape Fear (1961) (John MacDonald) Book/Movie (1991)

Whatever Happened to Baby Jane? (1962) Movie
Duel (1971) Movie
The Tenant (1976) Movie
Misery (1990) (Stephen King) Book/Movie
The Silence of the Lambs (1991) (Thomas Harris) Book/Movie

Racism as Monster

Broken Arrow (1950) Movie
Bad Day at Black Rock (1954) Movie
To Kill a Mockingbird (1963) (Harper Lee) Book/Movie
Little Big Man (1970) (Thomas Berger) Book/Movie
Pow Wow Highway (1989) Movie
Schindler's List (1993) (Thomas Keneally) Book/Movie
Rosewood (1996) Movie
Amistad (1997) Movie
The Pianist (2002) Movie

War as Monster

All Quiet on the Western Front (1930) (Erich Maria Remarque) Book/Movie
Grand Illusion (1937) Movie
Lifeboat (1944) Movie
The Red Badge of Courage (1951) (Stephen Crane) Book/Movie
Dr. Strangelove (1964) Movie
Shenandoah (1965) Movie
King of Hearts (1966) Movie
Catch-22 (1970) (Joseph Heller) Book/Movie
The Deer Hunter (1978) Movie
Apocalypse Now (1979) Movie (Loosely based on *Heart of Darkness* by Joseph Conrad)
Platoon (1986) Movie
Glory (1989) Movie
Henry V (William Shakespeare) Play/Movies (1944; 1989)
Three Kings (1999) Movie

Politics as Monster

Richard III (William Shakespeare) Play/Movies (1955; 1995)
Mr. Smith Goes to Washington (1939) Movie
All the King's Men (1949) (Robert Penn Warren) Book/Movie (2006)
Advice and Consent (1962) (Allen Drury) Book/Movie
The Manchurian Candidate (1962) (Richard Condon) Book/Movies (1962; 2004)

The Best Man (1964) (Gore Vidal) Play/Movie
Dr. Strangelove (1964) Movie
Seven Days in May (1964) (Fletcher Knebel & Charles Bailey) Book/Movie
All the President's Men (1976) (Carl Bernstein & Robert Woodward) Book/Movie
Winter Kills (1979) Movie
Nixon (1995) Movie

Power as Monster

Little Caesar (1930) Movie
The Public Enemy (1931) Movie
Scarface (1931; 1983) Movies
Citizen Kane (1941) Movie
One Flew Over the Cuckoo's Nest (1975) (Ken Kesey) Book/Movie
The Stunt Man (1980) movie
Bugsy (1991) Movie
Swimming With Sharks (1994) Movie

Economics as Monster

Oliver Twist (1838) (Charles Dickens) Book/Many Movies
The Grapes of Wrath (1940) (John Steinbeck) Book/Movie
An American Tragedy (1951) (Theodore Dreiser) Book/Movie: *A Place in the Sun*
Trading Places (1983) Movie
Erin Brockovich (2000) Movie
Match Point (2005) Movie

Family as Monster

Romeo and Juliet (William Shakespeare) Play/Many Movies
Hamlet (William Shakespeare) Play/Many Movies
King Lear (William Shakespeare) Play/Many Movies
East of Eden (1954) (John Steinbeck) Book/Movie
Cat on a Hot Tin Roof (1958) (Tennessee Williams) Play/Movie
The Fall of the House of Usher (1840) (Edgar Allan Poe) Story/Movie (1960)
The Manchurian Candidate (1962) (Richard Condon) Book/Movies (1962; 2004)
What Ever Happened to Baby Jane? (1962) Movie
Where's Poppa? (1970) Movie
Cries and Whispers (1972) Movie
The Godfather (1969) (Mario Puzo) Book/Movies: *The Godfather* (1972), *The Godfather II* (1974)

The Great Santini (1980) (Pat Conroy) Book/Movie
Ordinary People (1980) (Judith Guest) Book/Movie
Parents (1989) Movie
The Prince of Tides (1991) (Pat Conroy) Book/Movie

Aging as Monster

The Picture of Dorian Gray (1891) (Oscar Wilde) Book/Movie (1945)
King Lear (William Shakespeare) Play/Many Movies
Death of a Salesman (1949) (Arthur Miller) Play/Movie (1985)
All About Eve (1951) Movie
The Shootist (1976) Movie
The Grey Fox (1983) Movie
Death Becomes Her (1992) Movie

Religion/Church as Monster

The Hunchback of Notre Dame (1831) (Victor Hugo) Book/Many
    Movies
I Walked With a Zombie (1943) Movie (Loosely based on *Jane Eyre*)
Night of the Hunter (1955) Movie
The Conqueror Worm (1968) Movie
Carrie (1976) (Stephen King) Book/Movie

Image as Monster

Alice Adams (1935) (Booth Tarkington) Book/Movie
The Magnificent Ambersons (1942) (Booth Tarkington) Book/Movie
An American Tragedy (1931) (Theodore Dreiser) Book/Movie: *A
    Place in the Sun* (1951)
Mommie Dearest (1978) (Christina Crawford) Book/Movie (1981)
Working Girl (1988) Movie
The Heathers (1989) Movie
*The Positively True Adventures of the Alleged Texas Cheerleader-
    Murdering Mom* (1993) Movie
To Die For (1995) Movie

Disease as Monster

Panic in the Streets (1950) Movie
The Masque of the Red Death (1842) (Edgar Allan Poe) Short Story/
    Movie (1965)
Longtime Companion (1990) Movie
Philadelphia (1993) Movie
Outbreak (1994) Movie
12 Monkeys (1995) Movie

Consumerism as Monster

Fun With Dick and Jane (1977) (2005) Movies
Lost in America (1985) Movie

Sexuality as Monster

Madame Bovary (1949) (Flaubert) Book/Many Movies
Double Indemnity (1944) (James M. Cain) Book/Movie
The Postman Always Rings Twice (1946; 1981) (James M. Cain) Book/Movie
Alfie (1966; 2005) Movies

Obsession as Monster

Anna Karenina (1877) (Leo Tolstoy) Book/Many Movies
Greed (1924) (Frank Norris) Book/Movie
The Phantom of the Opera (1925) (Gaston Leroux) Book/Many Movies
The Maltese Falcon (1941) (Dashiell Hammett) Book/Movie
Laura (1944) (Vera Caspary) Book/Movie
Treasure of the Sierra Madre (1948) (B. Traven) Book/Movie
Sunset Boulevard (1950) Movie
The Searchers (1956) Movie
Vertigo (1958) Movie
Aguirre, the Wrath of God (1972) Movie
The Mosquito Coast (1986) (Paul Theroux) Book/Movie

Fear/The Unknown as Monster

The Haunting of Hill House (1959) (Shirley Jackson) Book/Movie: *The Haunting* (1963)
The Blair Witch Project (1999) Movie

Addiction as Monster

A Star Is Born (1937; 1954; 1976) Movies
The Lost Weekend (1945) (Charles R Jackson) Book/Movie
Days of Wine and Roses (1962) Movie
Long Day's Journey Into Night (1962) (Eugene O'Neill) Play/Movie
Papa's Delicate Condition (1963) Movie

Book Contract

Name
Date

After exploring ideas for this project with my classmates and visiting the library (choose one of the following types of monsters):

I am interested in a **literary** monster.

  Title of novel:

  Author:

I am interested in an **abstract** monster.

  Subject:

  I am interested because

  I will find research in the following places:

I am interested in a **generic** monster.

  Monster:

  I am interested because

"I Am the One Who" Poem Instructions

In this poem, you describe your monster's personality or physical appearance by speaking in the voice of your monster.

1. Review the information you have collected about your monster.

2. Mark passages that describe your monster.

3. Speak as if you are the monster. Begin with the line, "I am the one who," and then add details about your monster's personality and physical appearance.

4. Your poem should be 10–15 lines long.

5. "I am the one who" is a phrase that will help you begin your descriptive poem about your monster. If you repeat it occasionally, your poem will gain rhythm. But you do not have to continue to use this phrase if you have discovered other ways for your monster to describe who he or she is.

6. Read your poem aloud. Decide if you need to replace or drop excess wording. Try to show who your monster is through description rather than just telling (show, don't tell). For example, "I am angry" might be replaced by "I am the one who pounds on the door."

7. When you are satisfied with your poem, type it up. Be prepared to introduce your monster by reading your poem to the class.

Found Poem Instructions

In a "found" poem, you select words from a piece of literature (fiction or nonfiction) that you are reading. You are working with words written by someone else. Here is how it works:

1. Select lines from your reading (anywhere in the text) that describe your monster's personality and physical appearance. You may pick complete sentences, phrases, bits of dialogue, or descriptive words.

2. Select 10–15 lines so you have enough text to develop your own poem.

3. Arrange these lines in an interesting order that describes your monster.

4. Read the lines aloud. Drop excess wording or rearrange a line if needed.

5. Try using one repeating line to emphasize an idea, create a mood, or add rhythm to your poem. Repeat the line at the beginning, middle, or end of each stanza or throughout the poem.

6. Read your poem again. Listen to the words. Do you need to drop excess wording? Add a phrase or a line?

7. Revise your poem and read it to a friend.

8. Revise it again if you need to and give your poem a title.

9. When you are satisfied with your poem, type it up. Be prepared to introduce your monster to the class by reading your poem.

Presentation Worksheet

I will use the following ideas in my presentation:

- Recite a poem describing my monster
- Provide a quote and commentary about my monster
- Play a brief musical sample and provide an explanation
- Display a graphic or work of art and provide an explanation
- Explain a battle from my monster's point of view
- Introduce a thesis and support it
- Compare an artist's conception of my monster with the author's description
- Provide background information you have discovered through your research about a contemporary abstract monster (war, poverty, disease, etc.) and develop a strategy for solving this issue
- Present an internal monologue from the monster's point of view
- Compare and contrast the monster and the protagonist
- Other:

I will need the following equipment for my presentation:
(TV, VCR, cassette, CD player, overhead, other)

Appendix D

"I Was Friends With . . ."

Sample Teacher's Calendar

"I Was Friends With . . ." Tentative Calendar

Monday	Tuesday	Wednesday	Thursday	Friday	Saturday
• Review student instructions • Brainstorm list of possible writers for project • Allow students time to look through textbooks for an author	**Visit school library** • Allow students time to browse • Help students find appropriate author	**Visit school library** • Allow students time to browse • Help students find appropriate author	• Return to classroom • Students share author and novel they pick with the class • Clarify requirements for the portfolio; focus especially on purpose of reading journal	• Discuss and develop a weekend plan • Send individual students back to the library to pick an author • Students read their novels for remainder of period • Keep reading journal	**Weekend plan** • Read novel and work on reading journal • Visit public or university libraries
• Check students' progress on novel and reading journal • Students read novel and keep reading journal	• Students read and keep reading journal	• Students read and keep reading journal	• Pass out sample calendars • Students continue reading book review • Assign two students to lead discussion of book review Friday • Students read book review • Students continue reading novel	• Student analyze the book review (see student-led discussion)	**Weekend plan** • Complete novel • Write a legible draft of book review on novel • Visit public or university libraries

Monday	Tuesday	Wednesday	Thursday	Friday	Saturday
• Peers evaluate book reviews • Students rework them during class • Typed book reviews due Wednesday	**Workday** • Students work on book review or begin reading an autobiography or biography of their authors • Keep reading journal	• Students turn in final draft of book review • Students continue reading biographical material • Pass out a sample of an annotated bibliography • Assign a student to review annotated bibliography on Thursday	• Student-led discussion of how to format an annotated bibliography • Students continue to read biographical material • Check students' progress, answer questions, clarify specific project requirements	• Return book reviews and discuss with class • Develop a weekend plan • Read biographical material; keep reading journal	**Weekend plan** • Read novel and work on reading journal • Visit public or university libraries
• Check students' progress • Revisit school library	**Workday** • Work on sections of portfolio	**Workday** • Work on sections of portfolio	**Workday** • Work on sections of portfolio	• Check students' progress • Develop weekend plan • Brainstorm ideas for presentation	**Weekend plan** • Complete reading and reading journal • Begin assembling packet

(Continued)

(Continued)

"I Was Friends With . . ." Tentative Calendar

Sample Teacher's Calendar

Monday	Tuesday	Wednesday	Thursday	Friday	Saturday
Workday	Workday	• Ask students to write out their idea for presentation and a "needs list"—overhead, tape recorder, VCR, etc.	• Students bring unfinished portfolios to class and spend the hour writing a letter of evaluation • Portfolios due tomorrow	• Annotated portfolios • Allow students to share portfolios with their classmates • Develop a weekend plan	**Weekend plan** • Work on presentation
• Check students' progress • Portfolios due Friday • Develop criteria for evaluating presentations • Practice presentations with a classmate	Presentations	Presentations	Presentations	Presentations	

Teacher's Project Checklist

- ☐ Block out a tentative project calendar.

- ☐ Collect books and other resources to help students choose an author.

- ☐ Speak to the school librarian and other teachers who might be a resource to students during this project.

- ☐ Provide an overview of the project to the class.

- ☐ Brainstorm a list of authors with the class (this will save time).

- ☐ Share projects from past classes if you have them.

- ☐ Visit the school library several times with students.

- ☐ Return to the classroom and provide time for students to share project ideas and resources.

- ☐ Organize small-group discussions to facilitate student commitment to an author.

- ☐ Ask students to fill out book contract.

- ☐ Each Monday, make a plan with your students about work expectations.

- ☐ Ask students to keep a record of their daily accomplishments on a calendar that you provide.

- ☐ Develop a weekend plan with your students each Friday.

- ☐ Use peer tutoring to help struggling students.

- ☐ Monitor student work frequently by signing off on specific assignments.

- ☐ Embed student-centered behaviors.

- ☐ Use skill-based assignments during the project (grammar, punctuation, documentation, annotated bibliography, book review format, etc.).

- ☐ Grade assignments as they are completed.

- ☐ Pick up the pace between portfolio due date and the development of the presentation. (Students need the momentum to complete their presentations.)

- ☐ Provide students with opportunities to improve assignments to work toward mastery.

- ☐ Set up a student resource bulletin board and table in the classroom.

Student Checklist

- ☐ I understand the project requirements.

- ☐ I have chosen an author to research and have filled out the book contract.

- ☐ I have found sufficient research material to complete this project.

- ☐ I have decided on my relationship to the author.

- ☐ I keep a calendar of assignments and due dates.

- ☐ During my research and reading, I keep a reading journal.

- ☐ I have completed the research assignments for my portfolio.

- ☐ I have completed the essay.

- ☐ I have completed an annotated bibliography.

- ☐ I have completed my letter of evaluation.

- ☐ My portfolio is a formal research document that is prepared and formatted correctly.

- ☐ I have given my presentation and read the peer evaluations.

- ☐ I have listened to my classmates' presentations and have evaluated them using criteria developed by the class.

- ☐ I have facilitated a student-led discussion or taught a mini lesson.

Book Contract

Name
Date

1. After brainstorming ideas for this project with my classmates and visiting the library, I am interested in becoming friends with _____ (author's name) because _____ .

2. In my preliminary search, I have found the following research materials (circle those that apply):

   - Novels
   - An autobiography or biography
   - The author's correspondence
   - Journals or diaries
   - Literary reviews

3. My relationship with the author will be that of (circle the one that applies)

   - Friend
   - Family
   - Journalist
   - Publisher
   - Critic
   - Other (please specify)
   - I cannot determine my relationship until I do more research.

Student Presentation Worksheet

Use this worksheet to plan your presentation. Remember to present it from the perspective of a friend to your author (or whatever relationship you have chosen). Choose one period, idea, or important event in your author's life to be the centerpiece of your presentation.

1. As a friend (or family member, etc.) of _____ , I will use the following presentation format:

   - A formal speech about the author from the perspective of a friend
   - A monologue by the friend of the author
   - An interview
   - A skit using class members
   - The hot seat (the class interviews the friend of the author)

2. I will focus on the following time period, idea, or important event in the author's life:

3. I will introduce my presentation by:

4. I will cover the following points in my presentation:

5. I will conclude my presentation by:

6. I will need the following supplies or equipment:

   - An overhead and transparencies
   - Computer, VCR, or DVD player
   - Other (please specify)

Use this space to jot down ideas or questions you need to ask your teacher.

Appendix E

Tracing the Protest Movement in America Through Song: A Scavenger Hunt

Sample Teacher's Calendar

Tracing the Protest Movement in America Through Song: A Scavenger Hunt

Monday	Tuesday	Wednesday	Thursday	Friday
• Review project instructions • Pass out blank calendars • Students choose to work individually or in pairs • Students pull song title out of hat • Brainstorm how to find song lyrics	• Pass out worksheet, "Thinking About Your Protest Song" • Research protest song in library • Assign roles for class discussion • Homework: complete worksheet	• Review research progress • Student-led discussion on worksheet	• Connect protest songs to people, organization, history • Library research • Find literature to match protest song era	• Read literature and begin reading journal • Develop weekend plan
• Plan week's project work on calendars • Pass out worksheet, "Questions for Class Discussion" • Work on answering worksheet questions • Read literature and keep reading journal	• Develop criteria for small-group discussions • Break into discussion groups • Assign discussion roles • Homework: complete worksheet	• Set up discussion table • Small groups read/work in reading journal • Each group takes turns discussing worksheet questions • Videotape small-group discussions	• Complete small-group discussions • Continue reading	• Brainstorm ideas for song review/essay • Read literature and complete reading journal • Plan weekend work
• Plan week's project work on calendars • Turn in completed reading journal • Read sample song reviews and discuss them	• Peer teaching (thesis development) • Students work on thesis and begin writing	• Writing day • Choose peer teacher (revision)	• Peer teaching (revision) • Continue writing • Homework: completed draft	• Revise song review/essay in groups • Choose peer teacher (editing) • Weekend plan: revise writing

Monday	Tuesday	Wednesday	Thursday	Friday
• List criteria for writing song review/essay • Choose peer teacher (thesis)				
• Plan week's project on calendars • Peer teaching (editing) • Peer edit writing • Homework: writing	• Writing day • Homework: complete song review/essay	• Turn in song review/essay • Brainstorm ideas for presentation • Homework: write memo explaining presentation idea	• Review and refine presentation ideas • Discuss where presentations will take place • Make a list of equipment needed • Work on presentations	• Presentation work day • Outside reading • Weekend plan
• Plan week's project on calendars • Presentation development	• Develop presentation criteria • Select volunteer group to use criteria to develop a rubric • Work on presentation	• Volunteer group presents rubric for class feedback • Return song reviews/essays and discuss	• Practice presentations • Collect equipment • Invite classes to watch	• Finalize presentations • Outside reading • Weekend plan: practice presentation
	• Presentations • Student evaluations using presentation rubric			• Write letter evaluating project experience

Teacher's Project Checklist

- ☐ Collect books and other resources that will help students choose appropriate authors.
- ☐ Block out a tentative project calendar.
- ☐ Speak to the school librarian, computer teacher, history teacher, and other personnel who might be involved with students completing this project.
- ☐ Provide an overview of the project to your students.
- ☐ Share student work from prior years if you have it.
- ☐ Provide students with a list of suggested authors (this will save time).
- ☐ Ask students to look for research materials in the classroom and at home before visiting the school library.
- ☐ Visit the school library with the class (probably more than once).
- ☐ Return to the classroom and ask students to share resources and ideas.
- ☐ Ask a student to contact public and university libraries for their hours.
- ☐ Plan the week's work, write it on the board, and discuss it with your students. Ask them to keep a calendar (provided by you) so they will know what is expected of them.
- ☐ Develop a weekend plan with your students each Friday.
- ☐ Configure students in groups for review, brainstorming, and peer tutoring.
- ☐ Monitor student work frequently by signing off on specific assignments.
- ☐ Periodically evaluate student-centered behaviors with students.
- ☐ Embed student-led discussions, peer tutoring, and the development of criteria and rubrics.
- ☐ Embed assignments on skills and ask students to teach for extra credit (grammar, punctuation, citation format, annotated bibliography, book review, etc.).
- ☐ Pick up the pace between the portfolio's due date and the development of the presentation. (Students need the momentum to complete their presentations.)
- ☐ Don't wait until the end of the project to grade, or you may find yourself buried in work to review. Grade assignments as you move through the project.

Student Checklist

☐　I understand the project requirements.

☐　I have pulled a song title out of the hat and am committed to this topic.

☐　I have found the song lyrics.

☐　I have found material on a related protest movement or leader.

☐　I have completed the worksheets.

☐　I keep a calendar of assignments and due dates.

☐　I have completed the timeline graphic.

☐　I have completed the song review or essay.

☐　I have completed an annotated bibliography.

☐　I have completed my letter of evaluation.

☐　My portfolio is a formal research document that is prepared and formatted correctly.

☐　I have given my presentation and read the peer evaluations.

☐　I have listened to my classmates' presentations and have evaluated them using criteria developed by the class.

☐　I have facilitated a student-led discussion or taught a mini lesson.

Protest Song List

I have not listed songs from later than the early 1970s because I want students to connect with historical events in the past. I recommend you make your own list if you have time. It is an interesting walk through American history and there are many good protest songs.

Boycott of British Cloth: "Young Ladies in Town" by Dr. Joseph Warren (1776)

Revolutionary War: "On Independence" by Jonathan Mitchell Sewall (1860)

Underground Railroad: "Follow the Drinking Gourd" Negro spiritual (1850)

Attempt to Free Slaves: "John Brown's Body" by Anonymous (1860)

Civil War (North): "Battle Cry of Freedom" by G.F. Root (1862)

Civil War (South): "Everybody's Dixie" by Albert Pike (1861)

Prohibition: "Marching Through Rumland" by Horace B. Durant (1884)

Women's Suffrage: "I'm a Suffragette" by M. Olive Drennan (1912)

Labor Movement: "Solidarity Forever" by Ralph Chapin (1915)

Labor Movement: "Workers of the World Awaken" by Joe Hill (1916)

World War I: "I Didn't Raise My Boy to Be a Soldier" by Alfred Bryan (1915)

Coal Miners: "I Hate the Company Bosses" by Sarah Ogan Gunning (1930s)

Dust Bowl Days: "Blowin' Down This Road" by Woody Guthrie (1930s)

Lynching of a Black Man: "Strange Fruit" by Lewis Allan (1940)

World War II: "'C' for Conscription" by Pete Seeger/Millard Lampell (1941)

Atom Bomb: "Old Man Atom" by Vern Partlow (1945)

Korean War: "Brother in Korea" by Lou Osborne (1950s)

McCarthyism: "Joe McCarthy's Coming to Town" by Joe Glazer (1951)

The Rosenbergs: "Julius and Ethel" by Bob Dylan (1983)

Civil Rights: "The Death of Emmett Till" by Bob Dylan (1962)

Civil Rights: "Talking Birmingham Jam" by Phil Ochs (1963)

Cold War: "I'm Standing on the Outside of Your Shelter" by Shel Silverstein (1962)

Conformity: "Little Boxes" by Malvina Reynolds (1962)

Vietnam: "I Feel Like I'm Fixin' to Die Rag" by Country Joe and the Fish (1960s)

The Draft: "Draft Dodger Rag" by Phil Ochs (1965)

Plight of Native Americans: "Now That the Buffalo's Gone" by Buffy Sainte-Marie (1960s)

Environment: "Big Yellow Taxi" by Joni Mitchell (1960s)

Feminism: "I'm Gonna Be an Engineer" Peggy Seeger (1970)

Student Worksheet: Thinking About Your Protest Song

Please answer the following questions with these ideas in mind:

What can you learn from your song? Think about its significance historically and politically, and discover where and when it was sung. Read the words and analyze them, and find a recording of the song. Photocopy the words to your protest song.

1. Who wrote the song?

2. Was the song adapted from an earlier version?

3. List the emotionally loaded words in the song.

4. What slang terms or organizations are referred to in the song?

5. Is the song a ballad or parody?

6. Did a particular musician make the song popular?

7. Is the song still sung today? If so, do you know it?

8. Who were the protesters?

9. What event or issue were they protesting?

10. Give a brief summary of the historical context that inspired the protest.

11. Can you identify a specific segment of the population that was concerned about the issue? If so, why were they?

12. What was the reaction to the protest?

13. Did something change because of the protest? (working conditions, environmental protection, an end to a war, etc.)

14. Were there any famous slogans or symbols relating to this protest or conflict? Famous figures? Proclamations or amendments to the Constitution?

15. Can you think of any protests that have occurred in the recent past related to your song?

16. During your research, have you come across books, articles, or songs about protest that might be helpful to a classmate?

Student Worksheet: Questions for Class Discussion

1. Collect two definitions of protest.

2. What is the difference between a protest song and a folk song?

3. Are there protest songs that you listen to today on the radio and on CDs?

4. What is the difference between protesting and breaking the law?

5. Are there times in history when protesters broke the law for good reason, or do you feel there is ever a valid reason to break the law? Please find examples from history or from current news articles that support your opinion.

6. Can people be trained for nonviolent protest? If so, how might they be trained?

7. How do the attitudes of law enforcement play a role in successful nonviolent protest? Can you find an example of a situation where law enforcement and protesters were able to maintain a peaceful protest? When was this not the case?

8. Do we need the test of time to understand the impact of a particular protest or protest movement?

9. What issues in the recent past have incited a national protest movement?

10. What do you think helps our country survive protests by its citizens?

11. Are there issues of enough significance that you would willingly protest against our government? If so, what are they? Please explain their importance to you.

References

Arnett, H. (1975). *I hear America singing! Great folk songs from the revolution to rock*. New York: Praeger.

Helfert, M. (2001, May 6). *History in song*. Retrieved September 15, 2004, from http://www.fortunecity.com/tinpan/parton/2/history.html

National Council of Teachers of English & International Reading Association. (n.d.). *Standards for the English Language Arts*. Available online at http://www.ncte.org/about/over/standards/110846.htm

Robinson, E. (Ed.). (1963). *Young folk*. New York: Simon & Schuster.

Secretary's Commission on Achieving Necessary Skills. (2006, March 9). *SCANS report*. Washington, DC: U.S. Department of Labor. Available online at wdr.doleta.gov/scans

Silber, I. (Ed.). (1971). *Songs America voted by*. Harrisburg, PA: Stackpole.

Silber, I. (Ed.). (1973). *Songs of independence*. Harrisburg, PA: Stackpole.

Twain, M. (2003). *The adventures of Huckleberry Finn*. New York: Barnes and Noble Classics.

The Vietnam War 25 Years After. (2000, April 20). *What's going on? An incomplete list of songs about Vietnam* (compiled by Phil Nel). Retrieved December 12, 2004, from http://www.cofc.edu/%7Enelp/vietnam_music.html

Index